DELICIOUS
QUICK BREADS
AND MUFFINS

DELICIOUS QUICK BREADS AND MUFFINS

DIMETRA MAKRIS

FAWCETT COLUMBINE · NEW YORK

For my Mother

ACKNOWLEDGMENTS

This book is dedicated to my mother, who has been an inspiration to me. She encouraged me to try my skills in the kitchen very early in life and to enjoy cooking. Her recipes and advice are a great part of this book.

I thank my father, who has always insisted on quality—especially in foods and the preparation of them—for his invaluable critique of recipes and his many excellent suggestions.

There are friends who will stick with you through anything and some of them are:

Diane Powell, who gave her valuable advice, recipes, ideas, and, most important, made me laugh a lot;

Marie Morse, who tested recipes, came up with unusual ingredients, and was constantly supportive;

Lynne Aikman, Francesca DeFazio, and Niki Lagonikos for tasting and tasting and giving their valuable opinions; and

Susan Wolf Rifkin for always being a good friend.

My thanks to my brother Bill, sister-in-law Joe Ann, Richard, and Ginger. They not only ate a lot of muffins and bread, but Ginger helped me in the kitchen while testing.

I wish to thank my editor, Ginny Faber, for her guidance and encouragement, and my thanks also to Michelle Russell for helping with many of the details of this book.

I thank my agent, Julian Bach, who bakes in his own way.

CONTENTS

INTRODUCTION • 1

BAKING EQUIPMENT • 4

TIPS FOR SUCCESSFUL RESULTS • 6

INGREDIENTS • 10

MUFFINS • 13

    BASIC FLOURS AND GRAINS • 15

    FRESH FRUITS • 29

    DRIED FRUITS • 42

    VEGETABLES • 46

    NUTS AND SEEDS • 50

    SPICES • 56

    SPECIAL TREATS • 59

QUICK BREADS • 63

    BASIC • 65

    FRUITS • 73

    FRUITS AND NUTS • 82

    NUTS AND SEEDS • 100

    VEGETABLES • 106

A SAMPLING OF OTHER BAKED GOODS • 113

SAUCES AND SPREADS • 123

APPENDIX: EQUIVALENT WEIGHTS AND MEASURES • 131

INDEX • 135

DELICIOUS
QUICK BREADS
AND MUFFINS

❧   ❧   ❧

INTRODUCTION

This is a book for experienced cooks who love the comforting act of baking, and for beginners who would like to master that craft. The muffins and quick breads here will fill your kitchen with irresistible aromas and delight your family without taxing your skills or your purse.

Many of the recipes are adaptations of those I baked with my mother when I was growing up and those that I have collected over the years from family and friends. Others come from sources that I can no longer trace—a clipping here or there, notes and educated guesses on a bread tasted and enjoyed in a restaurant. I developed some of the recipes because of my special fondness for a fruit (the kiwi, for instance), or a nut (the pistachio).

The breads and muffins have been tested in a variety of settings. Many of my friends and family have lent their kitchens, sense of humor, and help to this project. My mother has extended her patience and her kitchen on my many visits, my father has offered valuable advice, Marie Morse has given her suggestions and tested recipes for me, and my childhood friend Diane Powell has always been there to help in every way.

The recipes have been tested in a variety of settings, often in cramped apartment kitchens with little workspace and unreliable ovens. (For a while it was a poorly insulated 1939 Norge oven.) But this is all for the best, because if the recipes turn out well under those adverse conditions, then even the beginning cook with a less than ideal kitchen can take heart.

You don't need more than basic baking equipment for this book, nor any specialized knowledge. Just follow the recipes. Carefully. In fact, I've included a children's recipe because I think it is important to encourage children to help in the kitchen at an early age. Obviously they will need some supervision and help, especially when dealing with hot pans and a hot oven. My mother welcomed me to her kitchen and taught me the pleasures of cooking when I was quite young, and I have always been grateful.

For the most part, these recipes don't call for ingredients that will strain the budget. Fruits from all seasons are included here, and I urge you to use seasonal produce. Forget the strawberries in January (unless you live in California)—there are plenty of winter fruits to choose. And don't overlook the great variety of nuts and spices, many probably already at hand in your kitchen. Even leftovers can find new life in a muffin or quick bread.

Most of the breads call for unbleached flour or a combination of unbleached and other flours. The breads use moderate amounts of honey or sugar, and in some cases fresh fruit juices provide additional sweetness, but none is overly sweetened. In fact, when retesting the recipes I often cut the sugar by half, or even more, and found the results sweet enough. No one who taste-tested ever complained about a lack of sweetness. No artificial ingredients or preservatives are used. Nearly all the recipes calling for butter specify unsalted butter. And as with sugar, I cut the salt by half when testing the recipes with the same satisfactory results. I use chemical-free baking powder, which can be purchased in health-food stores, or you can make your own (see page 12).

Most of the muffin recipes can be prepared and baked

within an hour. The quick breads take longer to bake, but no more of your time to prepare.

These fruit and nut bread recipes will serve, I hope, to provide novelty in a meal as well as a healthful substitute for richer desserts and snacks. You can enjoy them morning, noon, or night, and they can go on a picnic or into a lunchbox by themselves or in sandwich form.

Finally, don't take the book too seriously. Baking should be fun. Try your hand at your own fruit/nut combinations. Change the spices if you feel like it. (But unless you are an expert, don't tinker with the proportions of liquid and dry ingredients and leavening.) You may hit on entirely new and delicious varieties. You and your guests are in for some treats.

BAKING EQUIPMENT

Cooking should be done with the best equipment that one can afford. Good pans, skillets, and knives are a long-term investment, and with proper care can last a cook a lifetime.

I happen to prefer stainless steel, porcelain-coated cast iron, and glass pans for most of my baking, but the choice is up to the cook. Look for equipment that is well made and well designed. Avoid any pan that seems too light in weight (it may warp) or one with fluting or crevices that look hard to clean. Always buy a piece that can be hung if you have the choice. It will give you flexibility in storage and ease of use—having pans within easy reach can save many unnecessary steps in the kitchen.

Following is a list of basic equipment for use with this book. Any recipe can be made from this list. It's nice if you have a standard mixer or a food processor, but you don't need one to bake any of these breads or muffins successfully.

- one or two 8½ × 4½ × 2½-inch loaf pans
- one or two 9 × 5 × 3-inch loaf pans
- muffin pans (either 4 pans holding 6 muffins each or 2 pans holding 12 muffins each)
- one 13 × 9 × 2-inch pan

- wire cake racks
- one 8-inch square pan (and, optionally, one 9-inch square pan)
- heavy duty baking sheets (two are better than one, preferably two different sizes)
- one 9- or 10-inch tube cake pan (optional)
- glass measuring cups in 1-, 2-, and 4-cup sizes
- stainless steel measuring cups in cup fractions
- measuring spoons
- assorted sizes of mixing bowls in stainless steel, glass, or earthenware
- flour sifter
- strainer
- wooden spoons
- biscuit cutter
- potato peeler
- lemon squeezer
- metal spatulas
- 2 or 3 rubber spatulas
- wire whisks, assorted sizes
- nut chopper
- portable hand mixer
- blender

TIPS FOR SUCCESSFUL RESULTS

- *READ THE RECIPE*—The very first step is to read through the recipe, not only to determine if the necessary ingredients are on hand, but to note any special procedures that may be required. Are there nuts to chop, carrots to grate? Only after a careful reading of the recipe should you proceed to the actual preparation. Nothing is more frustrating than launching on a recipe and discovering midway that you are missing a key ingredient.
- *PREPARE TO BAKE*—Gather together all the ingredients and equipment that will be needed. This includes not only the specified pan but the bowls, measuring equipment, beaters, spoons, and spatulas.
- *PREHEAT THE OVEN*—Make sure that the oven temperature is correctly set and that oven racks are in the proper position before you begin.
- *GREASE THE PANS*—Pans can be buttered as lavishly or as sparsely as you like, just so long as the inside surface is thoroughly coated. I prefer to use unsalted butter but the choice is up to you. The average bread pan will take about 1 to 1½ tablespoons of butter. If a muffin batter will not fill all the cups in your muffin

pan, do not grease the unused cups. Instead put a tablespoon or two of water in them. This will protect the pan and provide steam to moisten the baking muffins.

- *SPECIAL PROCEDURES*—If there are any special items, such as chopped nuts, grated carrots, or peeled and chopped fruit, you should prepare them before measuring ingredients.
- *MEASURING INGREDIENTS*—For dry ingredients you need nested metal or plastic measuring cups from ¼- to 1-cup capacity; these should measure flush to the rim, enabling you to level off contents at the top. For liquid ingredients you need glass or plastic cup measures that have fractional markings visible from the outside, a margin at the top, and a pouring spout.

To measure powdered ingredients by spoon, first break up small lumps, fill measuring spoon to overflowing, then level off with the straight edge of a spatula or knife.

- *METHOD*—For best results in all recipes, butter, eggs and milk should stand at room temperature a short time before you use them. However, if separated eggs are needed, do the job while the eggs are still cold, and then let the whites and yolks stand. (Cold eggs separate more easily, but you will get more volume from your beaten egg whites if they have warmed up.)

All the recipes list the ingredients in their order of use, usually with the preparation of dry ingredients listed first. The entire mixing process will be faster and tidier if you measure all ingredients before starting the actual preparation. In recipes that call for sifted dry ingredients to be added to liquid ingredients, you can eliminate a bowl or two to wash by sifting onto wax paper.

- *MIX*—This is an especially important step in the preparation of nonyeast breads, and the procedure varies. The batters for many quick breads need to be thoroughly beaten to produce an even crumb in the finished loaf. On the other hand, most muffin recipes require the lightest possible touch in their mixing—

just a few quick strokes to moisten the dry ingredients. If a few lumps remain, ignore them. They will vanish in the baking. Overbeating will produce leaden muffins, coarse-grained and full of holes. So be sure to follow the mixing instructions for these recipes with care.

- *BAKING*—Baking times given in the recipes may need to be adjusted to your particular oven. Use an oven thermometer to make sure that your oven is close to normal temperature settings. Muffins baked at too low a temperature will not rise much, while those baked at too high a temperature will rise unevenly. You want the lovely symmetrical muffin with a gently rounded top produced at a correct oven setting. Check the bread or muffins a few minutes before the estimated time to make sure they are not browning too much.

The loaf breads often crack across the top. There is nothing wrong if this crack appears. Breads without yeast tend to be heavier, and that sometimes causes this to happen. The slices will look fine, with an even crumb.

- *TESTING*—Most breads are best tested by inserting a wooden pick in the center of the bread. If the pick comes out clean, the bread is thoroughly baked. The muffin that springs back from a light tap is fully baked.
- *COOLING*—Breads should be allowed to cool in the pan for 10 minutes on a wire rack. Then they should be removed and allowed to cool thoroughly. Many of the breads need to rest 24 hours before being cut; otherwise they are crumbly.

Muffins should be allowed to cool for 5 minutes in the pans and then removed. Where noted they should be served warm.

- *FREEZING and STORING*—Most of the breads in the book will freeze well. Just be sure they are thoroughly cool and wrapped properly for freezing. The same holds true for the muffins. For breads I use freezer paper. For the muffins I use freezer bags. That way a couple of muffins can be removed at a time.

For defrosting, I allow the muffins to sit out for 15 to 20 minutes. Then I heat them in a slow oven (200 degrees) for about ten minutes. For the breads, a longer thawing time is needed. Bread can be sliced after thawing and heated in the oven or in a toaster-broiler.

INGREDIENTS

FLOURS:

1. *Unbleached flour.* When white flour is needed, this is the best choice. In many recipes a combination of unbleached flour and other wheat flours is specified. Such a mixture gives a lighter feel to the bread while adding the nutrients of the wheat flours. However, don't let the absence of unbleached flour on your pantry shelf discourage your urge to bake. All-purpose flour will serve very well in a pinch.
2. *Whole wheat flour.* Be careful when buying commercially packaged whole wheat flours. Read the labels. Frequently preservatives have been added to the flour. Try to find unrefined whole wheat flour, with the bran and wheat germ still intact. Whole wheat flour should always be stored in the refrigerator.
3. *Bran.* This is a by-product of the refining processes of whole wheat grain and can be bought in health food stores and some supermarkets. Look for real bran, preferably miller's processed, and don't confuse it with the many bran cereals on the market.
4. *Wheat germ.* This is considered the heart of the wheat grain. It is usually removed from the wheat during

the refining process because it contains fat, which reduces storage time. You can purchase it separately and add it to your breads; it is full of nutrients.

5. *Graham.* A type of whole wheat flour ground from hard wheat kernel with the bran left in, graham flour is very coarse. Graham flour and whole wheat flour can be substituted for each other.

6. *Chickpea.* Round dried peas, usually tan or brown in color, these are also known by the Spanish name of garbanzo. They are a staple in Middle Eastern cooking and the flour is usually used in cooking rather than baking. Some of the recipes in this book use a combination of chickpea and other flours. It is available in stores that carry Middle Eastern food products.

7. *Corn meal.* Whether you use white or yellow, try to get stone-ground corn meal. Keep it in the refrigerator.

EGGS:
These recipes are based on USDA-graded large eggs.

BUTTER:
Unsalted butter is specified in nearly all the recipes.

FRUITS AND FRUIT JUICES:
Whenever possible use the freshest possible fruit and always use freshly squeezed juices if you can.

MILK:
Use homogenized milk, either regular or low-fat.

YOGURT:
Only plain yogurt is called for in these recipes. You can buy it or you can make your own according to the recipe on page 125.

SOUR CREAM:

Use the freshest possible and avoid using brands with additives or preservatives.

BUTTERMILK OR SOUR MILK:

I use these interchangeably. If you have neither on hand, you can produce perfectly adequate sour milk by stirring a tablespoon of vinegar or lemon juice into 1 cup sweet milk and letting it stand 5 minutes.

BAKING POWDER:

If cream of tartar is available, make your own by using 2 parts cream of tartar with 1 part baking soda. Use the same amount the recipe specifies for commercial baking powder. Chemical-free baking powder is available in health-food stores.

SPICES:

Use the best quality available, and to insure freshness keep them in a cool place away from light. I have been known to store them in the refrigerator to ensure freshness.

NUTS:

If you can find them, always purchase nuts unpacked. Good quality nuts are sold in bulk in many health-food stores, cooperative food stores, Greek and Middle Eastern shops, and by mail order.

MUFFINS

BASIC FLOURS AND GRAINS

BASIC MUFFINS

¶ *The basic muffin recipe lends itself to almost infinite variations, as subsequent recipes will demonstrate. Master the simple techniques of muffin-making with practice on this recipe and then branch out. You may want to invent combinations of your own.*

12 MUFFINS

2 cups unbleached flour
¼ cup granulated sugar
1 tablespoon baking powder
½ teaspoon salt
1 cup milk
⅓ cup melted unsalted butter or vegetable oil
1 egg

Preheat oven to 400 degrees. Grease muffin pans.

Sift flour. Then sift again with sugar, baking powder, and salt into a large bowl.

Measure milk in a smaller bowl. Add melted butter or oil and egg. Beat with a whisk or fork to mix well.

Make a well in center of flour mixture. Pour in milk mixture all at once. Stir quickly with fork until all flour is moistened. Do not beat or overmix. There may be a few lumps. Disregard them.

Quickly spoon batter into muffin pans. Bake 20 to 25 minutes, or until tops are golden and a wooden pick inserted in center comes out clean. Cool slightly on a rack. Turn out and serve warm.

❦

BRAN MUFFINS

¶ Bran muffins would appear to be a simple, straightforward subject and their recipe a simple matter. Not so. Everyone has an opinion, it seems. Thus this recipe has been a collective effort. It is based on one I have used for many years after sampling it at a friend's home. I have also used some suggestions from my friend Leon Morse, an expert bran muffin baker if ever there was one.

24 MUFFINS

2½ cups unbleached flour, sifted (or a combination of unbleached flour and whole wheat flour, for example, 1 cup whole wheat flour and 1½ cups unbleached flour)
2½ teaspoons baking soda
 1 teaspoon salt
 1 cup boiling water
 1 cup unprocessed bran (see note)
 ½ cup firmly packed brown sugar
 3 tablespoons honey (clover is a good choice)
 ½ cup vegetable oil *or* ½ cup (1 stick) unsalted butter, melted (or a combination of the two)
 2 eggs, well beaten
 2 cups buttermilk
1½ cups bran morsels, such as Bran Buds

Preheat oven to 375 degrees. Grease muffin pans.

Sift together flour, baking soda, and salt. (If you are using whole wheat flour, add it after sifting other ingredients.)

In a separate bowl pour boiling water over the unprocessed bran. Set aside.

Cream sugar, honey, and vegetable oil and/or butter in a large bowl until light and fluffy. (See note below.) Add eggs to creamed mixture and blend well. Blend in buttermilk, bran morsels, and unprocessed bran. Stir until blended. Mix in dry ingredients.

This mixture can be stored in a glass jar or lidded container in the refrigerator for up to six weeks. Just dip out as much as you need to bake at any particular time.

Bake muffins for 20 minutes at 375 degrees.

OPTIONAL:
You may add nuts, raisins, or dried fruit to the batter just before baking. Do not store the mixture with the nuts, raisins, or fruit mixed in, however. Use ½ cup raisins, ½ cup dried fruit, or ½ cup nuts for every six muffins baked.

NOTE: Unprocessed bran is frequently referred to as "miller's bran." It can be found in health food stores. No commercial bran cereals should be used as a substitute in this recipe.

NOTE: If only vegetable oil is used with sugar and honey it will not produce a fluffy mixture. Blend thoroughly and then add one egg at a time and beat thoroughly after each addition.

BRAN MUFFINS WITH CREAM CHEESE AND ORANGE MARMALADE

¶ *While living in Ethiopia, Sharon and David Brostrom developed this recipe. Bran was readily available and orange marmalade was one of the few luxuries that they could find there. This recipe delights their guests at the Hickory Ridge House in Putney, Vermont, year round.*

12 SMALL OR 9 MEDIUM MUFFINS

Preheat oven to 400 degrees. Grease muffin tins.

Combine in a bowl:

1 egg, slightly beaten
1 cup milk
2 tablespoons unsalted butter, melted
1 cup bran (see page 10)

Let stand 15 minutes.

In another bowl combine:

1 cup flour
1 tablespoon baking powder
2 tablespoons granulated sugar
½ teaspoon salt

Add this mixture to the egg mixture in the first bowl and combine with a spoon, but do not overstir.

Fill buttered muffin tins half full of batter. Add a teaspoon of cream cheese and a dollop of orange marmalade to each. Then cover with remainder of batter. Bake for 25 to 30 minutes at 400 degrees, until tops spring back when lightly tapped.

CHICKPEA MUFFINS

¶ *This recipe and its variations are from Marie Morse, a truly innovative cook. She introduced me to the use of chickpea flour; although chickpeas were familiar to me from my childhood, I had never used the flour before. These muffins are an excellent accompaniment to any dinner meal, or they can be served warm with an icy salad for a luncheon.*

6 MUFFINS

¼	cup (½ stick) unsalted butter
2 to 3	small scallions, finely chopped
2	tablespoons chopped parsley
1	cup chickpea flour (see note)
¼	cup all-purpose flour
1½	teaspoons baking powder
½	teaspoon salt
1	egg
½	cup milk

Preheat oven to 425 degrees. Grease muffin pans.

Melt butter in a small skillet; do not allow to brown. Soften scallions in the melted butter. Keep temperature (or flame) low and add chopped parsley. Remove from heat and set aside.

Sift together into a bowl the chickpea flour, all-purpose flour, baking powder, and salt.

Beat the egg, add the milk, and stir to combine. Add the egg/milk mixture to the flour. Then add the melted butter, scallions, and parsley and stir just until blended.

Divide among muffin cups and bake at 425 degrees for 10 minutes. Then lower oven temperature to 375 degrees and bake for another 15 minutes. These are best served warm, fresh from the oven.

VARIATIONS:
There are limitless additions to be tried with this flour combination. You might use 1 tablespoon finely chopped

dill in place of the parsley, and add crisply fried and crumbled bacon along with either the parsley/scallion recipe above or the dill variation. Other herbs and vegetables can also be substituted.

NOTE: Chickpea flour can be found in most Middle Eastern grocery stores in larger cities.

❧

BASIC CORN MUFFINS

¶ *This is the basic corn muffin recipe. Do also try the variations that follow, or invent some of your own.*

12 MUFFINS

- 1 cup unbleached flour, sifted
- 1 cup corn meal, preferably stone-ground
- 1 tablespoon granulated sugar
- 4 teaspoons baking powder
- ½ teaspoon salt
- 2 eggs, slightly beaten
- 1 cup milk
- ¼ cup (½ stick) unsalted butter, melted

Preheat oven to 425 degrees. Grease muffin pans.

Sift together into a bowl the flour, corn meal, sugar, baking powder, and salt. Make a well in the center and add the eggs, milk and butter. Stir until batter is smooth.

Spoon batter into muffin pans and bake at 425 degrees for 15 to 20 minutes or until muffins are lightly brown. Serve warm.

❧

CHEESY CORN MUFFINS

¶ *Take a good corn muffin recipe, add a little cheese to it and the result is a tasty cheese corn muffin. These are best served warm and are a great addition to a weekend brunch.*

8 TO 10 MUFFINS

½ cup yellow stone-ground corn meal
1 cup unbleached flour
1 tablespoon baking powder
1 tablespoon granulated sugar
½ teaspoon salt
¾ cup milk
1 egg
1 tablespoon unsalted butter, melted
½ cup shredded cheese, preferably mild or medium sharp Cheddar

Preheat oven to 375 degrees. Grease muffin pans. (Since this recipe will not fill a dozen muffin cups, put a couple of tablespoons of water in each of the empty ones. This will protect your muffin tin and help to keep your muffins moist.)

Sift dry ingredients together. Gradually add milk and mix well.

Beat egg and add to batter. Add the melted butter and shredded cheese. Pour into muffin pans and bake for 25 minutes, until tops rebound when gently tapped.

BLUE CORN MEAL MUFFINS

¶ *Blue corn meal has been with us for hundreds of years but just recently has been rediscovered. It is popular in the Southwest, especially in New Mexico, and can be used alone or in combination with other corn meal or flours. Its dark, purplish blue kernels make a striking addition to any breakfast table and it combines well with a number of fruits, especially blueberries.*

12–14 MUFFINS

1 cup blue corn meal
½ cup yellow corn meal
½ cup unbleached flour, sifted
2 tablespoons brown sugar
1 tablespoon baking powder
½ teaspoon salt
2 eggs, slightly beaten
1 cup milk
¼ cup (½ stick) unsalted butter, melted
½ cup sour cream

Preheat oven to 425 degrees. Grease muffin pans.

Mix together the corn meals, unbleached flour, sugar, baking powder, and salt. In another bowl, stir the beaten eggs with the milk, unsalted butter, and sour cream. Pour the liquid mixture into the dry ingredients and stir just until the entire batter is moistened.

Spoon into muffin pans and let set for 10 minutes. Bake at 425 degrees for 15 to 20 minutes or until muffins spring back to the touch. Serve warm.

JALAPEÑO CORN MUFFINS

¶ *A most unusual combination—practically a meal in themselves what with carbohydrates, the protein and fat in two cheeses, and even vegetables! The jalapeños give these muffins a nice zing.*

12 MUFFINS

1 cup yellow stone-ground corn meal
1 tablespoon granulated sugar
1 teaspoon salt
1 cup unbleached flour, sifted
1 tablespoon baking powder
1 egg, slightly beaten
1 cup milk
½ cup (1 stick) unsalted butter, melted
1 cup niblet-style corn, well drained
1 cup cottage cheese

FILLING:

½ cup finely chopped jalapeño peppers
½ cup sharp Cheddar cheese, grated

Preheat oven to 425 degrees. Grease muffin pans.

Sift together into a large bowl corn meal, sugar, salt, flour, and baking powder. Add the egg, milk, butter, corn, and cottage cheese, and stir lightly, just to mix and moisten all ingredients.

Divide half of batter among the muffin pans. Now spread the chopped chiles evenly across the batter and cover with the grated Cheddar cheese. Pour remaining batter over top to seal.

Bake for 20 to 25 minutes or until golden brown. If any of the Cheddar melts down the sides of the muffin tins, these may be a bit tricky to remove, but carefully sliding a knife around the muffins should do the job.

RASPBERRY CORN MUFFINS

¶ *Francine Gindi generously shares the following recipe from Gindi Desserts. In addition to their two New York retail locations, Gindi sells their muffins and desserts to restaurants and other retail outlets.*

9 MUFFINS

½ cup (1 stick) softened unsalted butter
½ cup brown sugar
2 eggs
1½ teaspoons vanilla
½ teaspoon cinnamon
1 cup corn meal
1 cup unbleached flour
1½ teaspoons baking powder
½ cup sour cream
1 cup fresh raspberries

Preheat oven to 350 degrees. Grease muffin pans.

Cream butter and sugar in a large bowl. Add eggs and beat two minutes. Next add vanilla and cinnamon and blend thoroughly. Add corn meal, flour, and baking powder. Beat one minute. Add sour cream and beat another minute. Fold in raspberries very gently.

Divide batter into muffin cups and bake for 20 to 25 minutes until brown and firm to the touch.

VARIATION:
For apple-bran muffins substitute bran for corn meal and chopped apples for raspberries.

GRAHAM MUFFINS

¶ *This is an excellent way to vary the types of wheat included in a breakfast meal.*

12 MUFFINS

3 cups graham flour
2 teaspoons baking powder
1 teaspoon baking soda
¼ cup light brown sugar
1 tablespoon unsalted butter, melted
1 cup sour milk
3 eggs, separated

Preheat oven to 400 degrees. Grease muffin pans.

Sift together flour, baking powder, and baking soda. Add brown sugar and mix in thoroughly.

Beat the egg yolks slightly and add to flour mixture. Mix in milk and melted butter.

Beat the egg whites until they hold stiff peaks and gently fold them into the batter.

Spoon into muffin pans and bake for 25 minutes. Cool for 5 minutes on a wire rack and remove from pans. Serve warm with butter or a homemade preserve.

OATMEAL MUFFINS

¶ *These muffins are best served warm with a homemade jam or apple butter.*

12 Muffins

1 cup unbleached flour
1 tablespoon baking powder
½ teaspoon salt
½ cup whole wheat flour
¾ cup rolled oats
¼ cup ground filberts or other nuts
1 cup milk
1 egg
3 tablespoons unsalted butter, melted
2 tablespoons honey

Preheat oven to 400 degrees. Grease muffin pans.

Sift together the unbleached flour, baking powder, and salt. Add the whole wheat flour, rolled oats, and ground nuts to the flour mixture and stir to mix well.

In a large bowl, beat together the milk, egg, melted butter, and honey. Add the flour mixture to the liquid and stir just until well blended.

Spoon batter into muffin pans and bake for 20 minutes or until muffins rebound when gently tapped. Serve warm.

ORANGE WHEAT MUFFINS

¶ *Although some may prefer to use all whole wheat for these muffins, I like using the combination of flours for a lighter result.*

12 MUFFINS

1   cup unbleached flour, sifted
2   teaspoons baking powder
½   teaspoon salt
1   cup whole wheat flour
½   cup firmly packed dark brown sugar
½   cup orange juice
½   cup milk
3   tablespoons grated orange rind
2   eggs, beaten
¼   cup (½ stick) unsalted butter, melted
½   teaspoon almond extract

Preheat oven to 350 degrees. Grease muffin pans.

Sift together the unbleached flour, baking powder, and salt. Add the whole wheat flour and brown sugar and blend well.

Combine in a separate bowl the orange juice, milk, grated orange rind, eggs, melted butter, and almond extract. Beat the mixture until well blended. Stir the liquids into the dry ingredients just until they are moistened. Do not overmix. Batter will be lumpy.

Spoon into muffin pans and bake for 20 minutes at 350 degrees until golden brown. Serve warm.

RICE MUFFINS

¶ *Here's a way to use that leftover cooked rice that so often languishes in the refrigerator for a few days and then gets thrown away.*

12 MUFFINS

- 1 cup unbleached flour, sifted
- 1 teaspoon baking powder
- 1 tablespoon granulated sugar
- ¼ teaspoon salt
- 2 eggs, beaten
- ½ cup milk
- ¼ cup (½ stick) unsalted butter, melted
- 1 cup leftover boiled rice

Preheat oven to 375 degrees. Grease muffin pans.

Sift together into a bowl the flour, baking powder, sugar, and salt.

Mix together the beaten eggs, milk, and melted butter in another bowl. Pour the liquid ingredients into the flour and stir briefly until just blended. Do not overmix. Fold in the rice thoroughly, making sure it is distributed throughout the batter.

Spoon into muffin pans and bake for 15 to 20 minutes. Cool for 5 minutes before removing from pans, and serve with a main meal.

VARIATIONS:
To vary these muffins add ¼ cup pine nuts or 3 tablespoons chopped parsley or another herb to the batter just before spooning into muffin pans.

FRESH FRUITS

APPLE MUFFINS

12 MUFFINS

2 cups unbleached flour, sifted before measuring
½ cup granulated sugar
½ teaspoon salt
1 tablespoon baking powder
½ teaspoon cinnamon
¼ teaspoon nutmeg
½ cup (1 stick) unsalted butter
1 egg
1 cup milk
1 cup grated apples

Preheat oven to 375 degrees. Grease muffin pans.

Sift together flour, sugar, salt, baking powder, cinnamon, and nutmeg. Set aside.

In a large bowl cream the butter, then add the egg and blend thoroughly. Add milk to butter/egg mixture and mix well. It may look curdled; that's all right.

Add the sifted dry ingredients to the liquid mixture and stir until blended. Fold in apples.

Spoon batter into muffin pans and bake for 30 minutes, or until the tops spring back when lightly tapped. Cool on rack for 5 minutes and remove from pans.

APPLE CHEESE MUFFINS

¶ *These muffins can be served any time. They are a delightful addition to a breakfast table, go especially well with luncheon salads, and can be served equally well with dinner. And they are packed with nutritious things!*

12 MUFFINS

½ cup (1 stick) unsalted butter
½ cup granulated sugar
 2 eggs
1½ cups unbleached flour, sifted before measuring
 1 teaspoon baking powder
 1 teaspoon baking soda
½ teaspoon salt
¾ cup quick-cooking (not instant) rolled oats
 1 cup finely chopped apples
⅔ cup coarsely grated sharp Cheddar cheese
¾ cup milk
12 thin slices apple

Preheat oven to 400 degrees. Grease 12 muffin pans.

In a large bowl, cream butter and sugar until light and fluffy. Add eggs, one at a time, beating well after each addition.

Sift flour, baking powder, baking soda, and salt onto wax paper.

Stir dry ingredients into butter mixture. Stir in oats, apples, and cheese. Mix well. Add milk gradually, stirring only to moisten other ingredients.

Fill muffin pans. Press 1 slice apple into the batter in each muffin cup. Apple slice should be completely covered by batter.

Bake for 20 to 25 minutess, or until tops spring back. Cool on rack for 5 minutes and remove from pan.

BANANA-DATE MUFFINS

¶ *These fragrant muffins can start the day off with a breakfast of eggs. Serve them plain or with one of the honey butters on page 128.*

12 MUFFINS

2 cups unbleached flour, sifted
1 tablespoon baking powder
½ teaspoon salt
2 tablespoons granulated sugar
1 egg, beaten
1 cup milk
¼ cup (½ stick) unsalted butter, melted
½ cup chopped dates
⅔ cup diced banana

Preheat oven to 425 degrees. Grease muffin pans.

Sift together into a large bowl flour, baking powder, salt, and sugar. Add beaten egg, milk, and melted butter. Gently mix in dates and bananas until thoroughly moistened. Do not overmix.

Spoon into muffin pans and bake for 20 to 25 minutes until golden brown and resilient to the touch. Cool for 5 minutes and remove from pans. Serve warm.

BLUEBERRY MUFFINS 1

¶ *One of the most popular muffin recipes is for blueberry muffins. Therefore, I have included more than one.*

12 MUFFINS

2 cups unsifted, unbleached flour
½ cup granulated sugar
1 tablespoon baking powder
½ teaspoon salt
1 cup fresh blueberries
1 cup milk
⅓ cup unsalted butter, melted
1 egg, slightly beaten
1 tablespoon grated lemon peel

Preheat oven to 400 degrees. Grease muffin pans.

In a large bowl, combine flour with sugar, baking powder, and salt. Stir in blueberries. In another bowl, combine milk, butter, and egg and beat with a fork. Make a well in center of flour-blueberry mixture. Pour in liquid mixture all at once. Add lemon peel. Stir quickly with a fork just until dry ingredients are moistened. Batter will be lumpy. Do not overmix.

Pour batter into muffin tins and bake at 400 degrees for 20 to 25 minutes until golden. Allow to cool for 3 minutes before removing from pans.

BLUEBERRY MUFFINS 2

¶ During a visit to Cape Cod a few years ago, one of the delightful inns we visited was The Village Inn at Yarmouth Port. Esther Hickey has graciously shared her delicious blueberry muffin recipe with me. Although she uses a muffin mix to speed up the many batches of muffins baked each morning, I have converted her recipe to use standard ingredients.

18 MUFFINS

2½ cups flour, sifted
  1 tablespoon baking powder
½ teaspoon salt
  1 scant cup granulated sugar
  3 tablespoons cooking oil (polyunsaturated)
  1 teaspoon pure almond extract
  2 cups fresh blueberries
  1 egg, beaten
1¼ cups whole milk

Preheat oven to 400 degrees. Place paper muffin cups in muffin tins (or grease muffin pans).

Sift together flour, baking powder, salt, and sugar. Add oil, almond extract, and blueberries. Add egg and milk and stir together. Do *not* beat.

Pour batter into muffin tins and bake at 400 degrees for approximately 20 minutes until golden.

CHERRY MUFFINS

¶ *Cherry muffins are a special yet very simple way to use those first cherries of the season. They are especially good served with fresh cream cheese. This recipe can easily be doubled.*

12 MUFFINS

- 2 cups unbleached flour, sifted
- 1 tablespoon baking powder
- ½ teaspoon salt
- 3 tablespoons granulated sugar
- 1 egg, well beaten
- 1 cup milk
- 3 tablespoons unsalted butter, melted
- ¾ cup fresh cherries, pitted and chopped

Preheat oven to 425 degrees. Grease muffin pans.

Sift together flour, baking powder, salt, and sugar. Sift a second time into a large bowl.

Combine the beaten egg with the milk and melted butter. Add the liquid to the flour mixture, stirring only until blended. Do not overmix. Fold in cherries.

Spoon the batter into greased muffin pans, filling them about two-thirds full. Bake for 20 to 30 minutes at 425 degrees. Keep an eye on them during the last few minutes of baking. This is a high temperature, and you don't want them overbrowned. Cool on a rack and then remove from pans.

CRANBERRY MUFFINS

¶ *This is a simple cranberry muffin with a touch of sugar to offset the tartness of the cranberries. They are quick to make and can be frozen and reheated without loss of flavor.*

12 MUFFINS

1 cup cranberries
⅓ cup confectioner's sugar
2 cups unbleached flour, sifted
2 teaspoons baking powder
½ teaspoon salt
⅓ cup granulated sugar
1 egg, beaten lightly
1 cup milk
3 tablespoons unsalted butter, melted

Preheat oven to 400 degrees. Grease muffin pans.

Pick over, wash, and drain cranberries. Sprinkle with confectioner's sugar and set aside.

Sift flour, baking powder, salt, and granulated sugar together. Sift a second time, into a large bowl.

Stir beaten egg into milk and then stir in melted butter.

Combine flour and milk mixtures, stirring as little as possible, just enough to moisten dry ingredients. Fold in cranberries and spoon into muffin pans at once.

Bake 20 to 25 minutes, cool briefly on rack, and remove from pans.

GRAPEFRUIT MUFFINS

¶ *These tangy muffins make an unusual addition to the breakfast menu. They are also good to serve at a brunch with sausage and eggs.*

12 TO 16 MUFFINS

½ cup (1 stick) unsalted butter
½ cup granulated sugar
2 eggs, beaten
3 cups minus two tablespoons unbleached flour
2 teaspoons baking powder
1 teaspoon salt
1 cup milk
¼ teaspoon baking soda
1 cup grapefruit sections, seeded and cut into small pieces

Preheat oven to 350 degrees. Grease muffin pans.

Cream butter in a large bowl until light and fluffy. Add sugar and blend thoroughly. Add beaten eggs.

Sift flour. Then sift together the flour, baking powder, and salt. Sift the three ingredients a second time.

Alternately add the sifted dry ingredients and the milk to the creamed mixture, beating well after each addition.

In a separate bowl sprinkle the baking soda over the grapefruit sections and toss to mix. Gently fold into the muffin batter. Pour into muffin pans and bake for 30 minutes, or until the tops rebound to your touch.

LEMON MUFFINS

¶ *These muffins are a nice addition to any meal and are especially enjoyable served with a salad for a luncheon. They can also be split and toasted.*

9 MUFFINS

2 lemons (approximately) for 1½ tablespoons grated lemon peel and 3 tablespoons lemon juice
1 cup unbleached flour
1 teaspoon baking powder
¼ teaspoon salt
½ cup (1 stick) unsalted butter
½ cup granulated sugar
2 eggs, separated

Preheat oven to 375 degrees. Grease muffin pans.

Grate lemon to yield 1½ tablespoon lemon peel. Then squeeze lemon and measure 3 tablespoons lemon juice. Set aside.

Sift and measure the flour. Then sift again with the baking powder and salt.

Cream the butter well. Add sugar gradually and beat until light and fluffy.

Beat the egg yolks until they are a light, lemon color and add to the creamed mixture. Add the flour mixture alternately with the lemon juice, mixing only until thoroughly blended. Do not overmix.

Beat egg whites until stiff but not dry. Gently fold egg whites and lemon peel into the batter.

Fill muffin pans three-quarters full. (Put a few tablespoons of water in the unused muffin cups.) Bake for 20 to 25 minutes or until a wooden pick comes out clean. Cool for 10 minutes on a rack and remove from muffin pans.

VARIATION:
To make orange muffins, substitute the same amount of grated orange peel and orange juice for lemon peel and juice.

PEACH MUFFINS

¶ *These muffins are a wonderful way to use summer's bounty of fresh peaches, and you'll want to try them with nectarines or pears, too.*

12 MUFFINS

2 cups minus 2 tablespoons unbleached flour
1 tablespoon baking powder
¼ teaspoon baking soda
⅛ teaspoon allspice
⅓ cup dark brown sugar, firmly packed
1 egg, beaten
1 cup sour cream
⅓ cup unsalted butter, melted
⅔ cup peeled and chopped fresh ripe peaches

Preheat oven to 400 degrees. Grease 12 muffin cups.

Sift and measure flour. Add baking powder, baking soda, and allspice and sift twice more, doing the last sifting into a large bowl. Add brown sugar and mix in thoroughly.

Stir beaten egg into sour cream and then mix in melted butter. Add the egg mixture to the dry ingredients, stirring just enough to moisten thoroughly. Add the chopped peaches, again stirring only until mixed. Batter will be lumpy. Do not overmix. All mixing can and should be done by hand.

Fill muffin cups two-thirds full and bake for 25 minutes or until golden brown.

VARIATIONS:

For *nectarine muffins* use ⅔ cup peeled and chopped fresh nectarines and follow recipe exactly as for peach muffins. To make *pear muffins* use ⅔ cup peeled and chopped fresh pears, and substitute ¼ teaspoon powdered ginger for the allspice if you wish. Always use ripe fruit for this recipe.

❦

PEAR MUFFINS

¶ *Pears are not usually associated with muffins, but why not use them? They are plentiful in seasons when berries and other perishable fruits are expensive. This is a good time to experiment with spices; a bit of cloves or nutmeg may suit you better than the cinnamon.*

12 MUFFINS

2 cups unbleached flour, sifted
1 teaspoon baking powder
½ teaspoon baking soda
¼ teaspoon salt
¼ teaspoon cinnamon
¼ teaspoon allspice
½ cup (1 stick) unsalted butter, softened
½ cup granulated sugar
2 eggs
½ cup plain yogurt
½ cup milk
1 cup peeled and chopped ripe pears
½ teaspoon almond extract

Preheat oven to 400 degrees. Grease muffin pans.

Sift together the flour, baking powder, baking soda, salt, cinnamon, and allspice.

In a large bowl cream the butter, add the sugar, and beat until fluffy. Add eggs one at a time, beating after each addition. Add dry ingredients to creamed mixture alternately with yogurt and milk. Gently stir in pears and almond extract.

Spoon into pans and bake for 20 to 25 minutes or until a wooden pick inserted in center comes out clean. Cool on a rack for 5 minutes and remove from pans. Serve warm, plain or with pear-cranberry butter.

PINEAPPLE-BACON MUFFINS

¶ This tangy, slightly salty combination makes a great start in the morning.

12 Muffins

- 3 strips bacon
- 1 cup unbleached flour, sifted
- 1 teaspoon baking powder
- ¾ teaspoon baking soda
- ¼ teaspoon salt
- 1 cup corn meal
- ½ cup drained crushed pineapple, or ½ cup diced fresh pineapple
- 2 eggs
- 1½ cups buttermilk
- 2 tablespoons brown sugar
- ¼ cup bacon drippings

Preheat oven to 425 degrees. Grease muffin pans.

Fry bacon until crisp. Drain on paper towel and crumble. Reserve ¼ cup bacon drippings.

Sift into a large bowl the flour, baking powder, baking soda, salt, and corn meal. Stir in pineapple.

Beat eggs. Add buttermilk, sugar, and reserved bacon drippings to eggs and beat together until smooth. Pour into flour mixture and stir only until flour is moistened.

Fill muffin pans two-thirds full. Sprinkle crumbled bacon on top of the batter. Bake for 20 to 25 minutes until nicely browned, cool briefly on a wire rack, and remove from pans.

STRAWBERRY YOGURT MUFFINS

¶ *Always use plain yogurt for this recipe. If you are adventurous you might consider trying your hand at making your own yogurt from the recipe on page 125.*

12 MUFFINS

1½ cups unbleached flour
¼ teaspoon salt
½ teaspoon cream of tartar
¼ teaspoon baking soda
½ cup (1 stick) unsalted butter
½ cup granulated sugar
½ teaspoon vanilla
 2 eggs
¼ cup yogurt
⅔ cup chopped fresh strawberries

Preheat oven to 400 degrees. Grease muffin pans.

Sift flour. Then sift together flour, salt, cream of tartar, and baking soda into a bowl.

Cream butter and sugar in a large bowl until fluffy. Add vanilla. Add eggs one at a time, beating well after each.

Alternately add dry ingredients and yogurt to creamed ingredients. Gently fold in strawberries.

Spoon into muffin pans and bake 25 minutes or until golden brown. Allow muffins to cool on a rack for 10 minutes before removing from pans.

VARIATIONS:
For *blueberry muffins* use 1 cup whole blueberries instead of chopped strawberries. To make *raspberry muffins* use ⅔ cup whole raspberries instead of chopped strawberries.

DRIED FRUITS

APRICOT-NUT MUFFINS

¶ *Use the best quality dried apricots you can find for these muffins.*

12 MUFFINS

½ cup dried apricots
1 cup water
1 egg
½ cup granulated sugar
2 tablespoons unsalted butter, melted
2 cups unbleached flour
1 tablespoon baking powder
¼ teaspoon baking soda
½ teaspoon salt
½ cup orange juice, preferably freshly squeezed
¼ cup water
⅔ cup chopped filberts

Soak dried apricots in 1 cup water for 25 minutes. Drain and dice.

Preheat oven to 350 degrees. Grease muffin pans.

In a large bowl, beat egg until light. Add sugar and blend well. Stir in melted butter.

Sift flour. Then resift with baking powder, soda, and salt.

Add flour to creamed mixture alternately with the orange

juice and ¼ cup water mixed together. Add the filberts and apricots and blend well.

Fill muffin tins with batter and bake at 350 degrees for 20 to 25 minutes, or until muffins are a golden color.

DATE MUFFINS

¶ *Other dried fruits can be substituted successfully for the dates here, but there is something comfortably old-fashioned and familiar about a date muffin. And, of course, they are delicious.*

12 MUFFINS

- 2 cups minus two tablespoons unbleached flour, sifted
- 2 teaspoons baking powder
- ½ teaspoon salt
- ¼ cup brown sugar
- 1 cup milk
- 1 egg, beaten
- ⅓ cup unsalted butter, melted
- 1 cup pitted and chopped dates

Preheat oven to 400 degrees. Grease muffin pans.

Sift together into a large bowl the flour, baking powder, and salt. Stir in brown sugar and mix well.

In a separate bowl add milk to the beaten egg and blend in melted butter.

Add the liquid ingredients to the flour mixture, mix quickly, and stir in dates. Spoon into muffin pans and bake for 20 to 25 minutes, until browned and springy to the touch. Cool on rack for 5 minutes and remove from pan.

FIG MUFFINS

¶ *Dried figs make a pleasant change from the familiar date muffins. These make a wonderful addition to a lunchbox.*

12 MUFFINS

1 cup unbleached flour, sifted
1 tablespoon baking powder
½ teaspoon salt
1 cup rolled oats
⅓ cup firmly packed brown sugar
1 egg, beaten
1 cup milk
3 tablespoons vegetable oil
½ cup chopped dried figs

Preheat oven to 400 degrees. Grease muffin pans.

Sift together the flour, baking powder, and salt. Add the oats and brown sugar and stir well.

In another bowl mix the egg, milk, and vegetable oil. Stir liquid into dry ingredients just until moistened. Fold in figs. Spoon into muffin pans, and bake for 15 to 20 minutes.

VARIATIONS:

Instead of figs, substitute ½ cup chopped dried pears, apricots, or peaches, or ½ cup stewed and chopped prunes.

PRUNE MUFFINS

¶ *The lowly prune, so often scorned, makes a marvelous muffin—and we all know how good prunes are for us.*

12 MUFFINS

2 cups unbleached flour, sifted
½ cup firmly packed brown sugar
1 tablespoon baking powder
½ teaspoon salt
¼ teaspoon nutmeg
¼ cup (½ stick) unsalted butter, melted
1 egg, lightly beaten
1 cup milk
¾ cup cooked, chopped prunes

Preheat oven to 400 degrees. Grease muffin pans.

Stir together in a large bowl the flour, sugar, baking powder, salt, and nutmeg. Add the melted butter, egg, and milk, and stir quickly to moisten the dry ingredients. Fold in prunes.

Spoon batter into pans and bake for 20 to 25 minutes, until resilient to your light tap. Cool on a rack for 5 minutes and then remove from muffin pans and allow to cool thoroughly.

VEGETABLES

CARROT-ZUCCHINI MUFFINS

¶ *Here is a combination of ingredients frequently on hand in many homes. It makes a good moist muffin, especially welcome in the morning, served warm.*

12 MUFFINS

1½ cups unbleached flour, sifted
1½ tablespoons baking powder
 1 cup whole wheat flour
 ¼ cup (½ stick) unsalted butter
 6 tablespoons (¼ cup + 2 tablespoons) honey
 ¼ cup orange marmalade
 1 large, peeled, grated carrot (½ cup)
 1 peeled, grated zucchini (½ cup)
 3 eggs
 ¾ cup milk
 1 teaspoon vanilla

Preheat oven to 325 degrees. Grease muffin pans.

Sift the unbleached flour and baking powder together and then mix in the whole wheat flour. Set aside.

In a small pan combine the butter, honey, and marmalade and heat the mixture over low heat until the ingredients dissolve. Allow to cool.

In a large bowl beat the eggs. Add the milk, carrot, zucchini, and honey/butter mixture. Add the vanilla. Mix in the dry ingredients, stirring only until ingredients are blended. Do not overmix.

Spoon batter into muffin pans. Bake for 30 to 35 minutes at 325 degrees, or until muffins spring back to a light touch. Cool in pans for 10 minutes, turn out, and serve warm.

❦

PUMPKIN MUFFINS

¶ *The pumpkin seeds in these muffins make them just a bit different from other pumpkin muffins and add a nice, crunchy texture. Obviously fresh pumpkin would be great, but you needn't feel compelled to raid the Halloween display. Canned pumpkin (not pumpkin pie filling) will do perfectly well. The recipe doubles well.*

10 MUFFINS

¼ cup (½ stick) unsalted butter, softened
½ cup firmly packed brown sugar
1 egg, slightly beaten
¼ cup buttermilk
⅓ cup cooked and mashed pumpkin
2 to 3 tablespoons pumpkin seeds, plus a few for garnish
1 cup unbleached flour, sifted
½ teaspoon salt
½ teaspoon ground cinnamon
¼ teaspoon baking soda
1½ teaspoons baking powder
⅛ teaspoon ground ginger
⅛ teaspoon ground mace

Preheat oven to 375 degrees. Grease muffin pans.

Cream butter and sugar together in a large bowl. Add beaten egg, buttermilk, and pumpkin and stir well. Mix in the pumpkin seeds.

In a bowl, sift together the flour, salt, cinnamon, baking soda, baking powder, ginger, and mace. Add the dry ingredients to the liquid mixture and stir just until moistened.

Spoon into muffin pans. Sprinkle a few pumpkin seeds on top of each muffin and bake for about 20 minutes or until a wooden pick inserted in center comes out clean. Remove from pan after 5 minutes of cooling on a rack.

SQUASH MUFFINS

¶ *Use whatever cooked squash you have on hand—another tasty way to profit from leftovers.*

12 Muffins

2 cups unbleached flour, sifted
2 teaspoons baking powder
¼ teaspoon salt
2 eggs, well beaten
1 cup cooked, mashed summer or winter squash
1 tablespoon butter, melted
1 cup milk

Preheat oven to 375 degrees. Grease muffin pans.

Sift together into a large bowl the flour, baking powder, and salt.

In a separate bowl mix the beaten eggs with the squash. Add to this the melted butter and milk and mix thoroughly. Add the liquids to the dry ingredients and stir just until they are thoroughly moist.

Spoon batter into muffin pans and bake for 25 to 30 minutes, until a tester inserted in one muffin comes out clean. Cool five minutes and serve with a salad or main course.

❦

ZUCCHINI MUFFINS WITH WHEAT GERM

¶ *These muffins are best served warm. They can be made in advance, frozen, and reheated in foil for about 15 minutes at 375 degrees. If your zucchini is young and tender, don't peel it. Just scrub and dry it thoroughly before shredding.*

12 MUFFINS

2 cups unbleached flour, sifted
1 cup shredded zucchini
⅔ cup wheat germ
½ cup firmly packed dark brown sugar
1 tablespoon baking powder
¾ cup milk
¼ cup vegetable oil
1 egg, beaten

Preheat oven to 375 degrees. Grease muffin pans.

Mix flour, zucchini, wheat germ, brown sugar, and baking powder in a bowl.

In another bowl stir together milk, oil, and beaten egg to mix well. Then stir the liquid mixture into the flour mixture just until blended. Do not overmix.

Spoon batter into muffin pans and bake for 20 to 25 minutes or until golden brown. Cool for 10 minutes and remove from pans. Serve warm.

NUTS AND SEEDS

HEALTH NUT MUFFINS

¶ *The name says it all. These chewy muffins are filled with everything we hear is good for us—wheat germ, wheat flour, fruit, nuts, orange juice, and more. How nice that anything so virtuous can taste so good.*

18 MUFFINS

½ cup unbleached flour, sifted
½ cup whole wheat flour
¼ teaspoon salt
¼ teaspoon baking soda
1 teaspoon baking powder
⅓ cup nonfat dry milk powder
¼ cup wheat germ
¼ cup firmly packed brown sugar
¼ cup chopped Brazil nuts
¼ cup raisins
1 large egg
¼ cup vegetable oil
¼ cup molasses
½ cup orange juice
¼ cup chopped dried apricots

Preheat oven to 350 degrees. Grease muffin pans.

Combine sifted unbleached flour, whole wheat flour, salt, baking soda, baking powder, dry milk, wheat germ, brown sugar, nuts, and raisins in a large bowl and toss well to blend thoroughly.

In an electric blender whip the egg until foamy. Add the oil, molasses, and orange juice one item at a time, blending after each addition. Add apricots and process just to chop coarsely.

Pour the liquid mixture into the bowl with the dry ingredients and stir just until all flour is moistened. Pour into greased muffin pans and bake for 20 minutes, until browned and firm to the touch. Allow to cool on a rack for 5 minutes and remove from pans.

MAPLE FILBERT MUFFINS

¶ *All too often we get into a cooking rut, always using walnuts or pecans, for example, when nuts are called for. Many other kinds of nuts can be included in a recipe, giving a unique flavor to the results.*

12 MUFFINS

1½ cups unbleached flour, sifted
 1 teaspoon baking soda
 ½ cup bran
 ½ cup chopped filberts
 1 cup sour cream
 ½ cup maple syrup
 2 eggs

Preheat oven to 400 degrees. Grease muffin pans.

Sift together into a bowl the flour and baking soda. Add the bran and filberts and mix thoroughly.

In a separate bowl combine the sour cream, maple syrup,

and eggs. Add to the flour mixture and stir until thoroughly moistened. Do not overmix.

Spoon into muffin pans and bake for 20 minutes, until nicely browned. Remove from oven and cool on a wire rack for 5 minutes. Remove from muffin pan and serve warm.

PECAN SPICE MUFFINS

12 MUFFINS

    2 cups unbleached flour, sifted
    ½ teaspoon salt
    4 teaspoons baking powder
    ¼ teaspoon nutmeg
    ¼ teaspoon cinnamon
    ¼ teaspoon cloves
    ¼ cup granulated sugar
    1 egg, beaten
    1 cup milk
    ¾ cup chopped pecans
    ¼ cup (½ stick) unsalted butter, melted

Preheat oven to 425 degrees. Grease muffin pans.

Sift together into a bowl the flour, salt, baking powder, nutmeg, cinnamon, cloves, and sugar.

Beat the egg and milk together in a large bowl. Add the sifted dry ingredients and mix lightly. Stir in the nuts and the melted butter.

Spoon the batter into pans and bake for 20 to 25 minutes, until golden brown. Cool on a wire rack for 5 minutes and remove from pans. Serve warm.

PINE NUT-RAISIN MUFFINS

¶ *This recipe from Marie Morse is another that uses chick-pea flour (see Chickpea Muffins). Serve these muffins for breakfast, or better still to ward off the midafternoon doldrums with a freshly brewed cup of tea or coffee.*

6 MUFFINS

    1   cup chickpea flour
    ¼   cup all-purpose flour
    3   tablespoons granulated sugar
  1½   teaspoons baking powder
    ½   teaspoon salt
    ½   cup milk
    1   egg, beaten
    ¼   cup (½ stick) unsalted butter, melted
    ¼   cup raisins
    2   tablespoons pine nuts

Preheat oven to 425 degrees. Grease muffin pans.

Sift together the chickpea flour, all-purpose flour, sugar, baking powder, and salt into a large bowl.

Combine the milk with the beaten egg and add to the dry ingredients. Then add the melted butter and quickly stir everything just until blended. Fold in the raisins and pine nuts.

Spoon batter into muffin pans and bake at 425 degrees for 10 minutes. Then lower oven temperature to 375 degrees and bake for another 15 minutes. Cool on rack for 10 minutes and remove from pans.

POPPY SEED MUFFINS

2 cups unbleached flour, sifted
½ cup granulated sugar
½ teaspoon salt
1 tablespoon baking powder
½ teaspoon mace
½ cup (1 stick) salted butter
1 egg
1 cup light cream
¾ cup peeled and grated apple
½ cup poppy seeds
2 tablespoons lemon rind

Preheat oven to 375 degrees. Grease muffin pans.

Sift together the flour, sugar, salt, baking powder, and mace.

In a large bowl cream the butter and then add the egg and blend thoroughly. Add the cream and stir well to blend. Add the dry ingredients and stir quickly until smooth. Fold in the grated apple, poppy seeds, and lemon rind.

Spoon batter into muffin pans and bake for 30 minutes or until browned and springy to a light tap. Cool on rack for 5 minutes and remove from pan.

SUNNY SEEDED MUFFINS

¶ *Sesame seeds, sunflower seeds, and almonds make this a crunchy, nutritious muffin, particularly good to pack for snacks, picnics, or lunchboxes.*

12 MUFFINS

1   cup unbleached flour
1   tablespoon baking powder
1   cup whole wheat flour
¼   cup toasted sesame seeds
⅓   cup toasted sunflower seeds
1   cup chopped almonds
1   egg, beaten
1   cup milk
4   teaspoons vegetable oil
4   teaspoons honey

Preheat oven to 400 degrees. Grease muffin pans.

Sift unbleached flour and baking powder together into a large bowl. Thoroughly mix in whole wheat flour. Stir in sesame seeds, sunflower seeds, and almonds.

In a separate bowl beat the egg and add the milk, oil, and honey. Pour the liquid ingredients into the dry and stir just until they are blended.

Fill muffin pans three-quarters full and bake for 10 to 15 minutes until a tester inserted in center of a muffin comes out clean. Cool on rack for 10 minutes and remove from pan.

SPICES

GINGER MUFFINS

¶ *This ginger muffin batter will keep up to 4 weeks in a closed glass container in the refrigerator. The recipe can be doubled and used whenever needed.*

12 MUFFINS

½ cup (1 stick) unsalted butter
¼ cup granulated sugar
2 eggs
¼ cup molasses
1 teaspoon baking soda
½ cup sour milk
2 cups unbleached flour
1 teaspoon ginger
¼ teaspoon cinnamon
¼ teaspoon allspice
¼ cup raisins

Preheat oven to 350 degrees. Grease muffin pans.

In a large bowl, cream butter, then gradually add sugar and continue to beat until fluffy. Add eggs, one at a time, beating well after each. Mix in molasses and stir thoroughly.

In a small bowl mix baking soda into sour milk. When it starts to foam, stir into creamed mixture.

Sift together flour, ginger, cinnamon, and allspice into another bowl. Gradually add flour mixture to liquid, mixing only until all ingredients are moistened. Fold in raisins.

Spoon batter into muffin pans and bake 20 minutes, or until tops of muffins spring back when lightly touched. Cool on a wire rack for 5 minutes and remove from pan. These muffins freeze well.

NUTMEG MUFFINS

¶ *Adapt this recipe to use any spice you choose. Clove, cinnamon, ginger, mace, or a combination of spices will make a simple and interesting muffin.*

12 MUFFINS

TOPPING:
- 1 cup unbleached flour
- ½ cup dark brown sugar
- 6 tablespoons unsalted butter

BATTER:
- ½ cup unbleached flour, sifted
- 1 teaspoon baking powder
- 1 teaspoon freshly grated nutmeg (ground nutmeg may be substituted)
- ½ teaspoon baking soda
- ½ teaspoon salt
- ½ cup sour milk
- 1 egg, beaten

Preheat oven to 350 degrees. Grease muffin pans.

Prepare the topping ingredients: Mix the 1 cup flour and the brown sugar thoroughly in a bowl. Cut in the butter until it resembles coarse meal. Remove and reserve ½ cup of the mixture for topping.

Add the remaining ½ cup flour, baking powder, nutmeg, baking soda, and salt to the coarse mixture, mix in the sour milk and egg, stirring until just moistened.

Spoon batter into muffin cups, filling each about one-half full. Sprinkle each muffin with 2 teaspoons of the topping. Bake for about 20 to 25 minutes or until a wooden pick inserted in center comes out clean. Cool on a wire rack for 5 minutes and remove from pans. These muffins freeze well.

SPECIAL TREATS

COCONUT MUFFINS

¶ *Some cooks may prefer to toast the coconut for these muffins, but they are enjoyable either way. They are especially good served warm.*

12 MUFFINS

1¾ cups unbleached flour, sifted
 ½ cup granulated sugar
 1 tablespoon baking powder
 ½ teaspoon salt
 1 cup fresh or canned flaked coconut, toasted if desired
 1 cup milk
 ¼ cup (½ stick) unsalted butter, melted
 1 egg, slightly beaten

Preheat oven to 400 degrees. Grease muffin pans.

Sift together flour, sugar, baking powder, and salt into a large bowl. Add the coconut and mix well.

In a small bowl stir together milk, melted butter, and egg.

Make a well in center of flour mixture. Pour in the liquid mixture all at once. Stir quickly with a fork, just until dry ingredients are moistened. Do not overmix. Batter will be lumpy.

Spoon into muffin pans. Bake 20 to 25 minutes until a golden brown. Cool for 5 minutes. Remove from pan and serve warm.

❦

COFFEE MUFFINS

¶ *What else but a hot cup of coffee to go with these muffins?*

12 MUFFINS

2 cups unbleached flour, sifted
1 tablespoon baking powder
½ teaspoon salt
⅓ cup firmly packed brown sugar
½ cup chopped pecans
½ cup strong coffee
½ cup light cream
1 egg, beaten
¼ cup (½ stick) unsalted butter, melted

Preheat oven to 400 degrees. Grease muffin pans.

Sift together into a large bowl the flour, baking powder, and salt. Mix in the brown sugar and pecans.

In a separate bowl stir together the coffee, cream, egg, and melted butter. Mix the liquid into the flour mixture all at once, but stir only enough to moisten all ingredients.

Spoon batter into muffin pans and bake for 20 minutes, until tops spring back when tapped. Cool for 5 minutes, then remove from pan and cool on wire rack, or serve immediately.

❦

MUFFINS WITH A SURPRISE

¶ *Muffins are a good way to introduce children to baking. Below is a recipe from my friend John Moore, age ten. John has shown an interest in cooking since he was five years old (or perhaps even earlier; at two years of age he added a cup of soapy water to his mother's cooking batter) and this muffin recipe is one he has mastered.*

12 MUFFINS

1¾ cup unbleached flour
¼ cup granulated sugar
2½ teaspoons baking powder
½ teaspoon salt
1 egg
¾ cup milk
⅓ cup vegetable oil
12 teaspoons grape jelly or apricot jam

Grease muffin pans. Preheat oven (with the help of an adult) to 400 degrees.

Measure and sift together flour, sugar, baking powder, and salt into a medium-sized bowl.

Use a fork to beat one egg in a smaller bowl. Add milk and vegetable oil and beat with a fork until blended. Pour milk mixture over the flour mixture and stir with a wooden spoon only until all flour is wet. Batter should be lumpy. Do not overstir.

Spoon half the batter into muffin pans. Each muffin pan should be about one-third full. Put 1 teaspoonful of grape jelly or apricot jam into each muffin cup. (A real surprise would be to fill one-half of the cups with grape jelly and one-half with apricot jam.) Then spoon remaining batter over the jelly or jam.

With the help of an adult place the muffin pans in the oven and bake for 20 to 25 minutes, or until muffins are golden. With the help of an adult remove the muffins from the oven and cool for 5 minutes on a wire rack. Using a spatula or butter knife, loosen the muffins and remove them from the pan.

❧

SALLY LUNN

¶ *According to folklore this muffin was named for the young woman in England who originated it. The traditional Sally Lunn is a towering golden yeast bread often baked in a tube pan, but there are a number of quick versions, of which this is one.*

12 MUFFINS

2 cups unbleached flour, sifted
½ teaspoon salt
2 tablespoons granulated sugar
4 teaspoons baking powder
¼ cup (½ stick) unsalted butter
3 large eggs, separated
1 cup milk

Preheat oven to 400 degrees. Grease muffin pans.

Sift together the flour, salt, sugar, and baking powder. Sift again, into a large bowl. Cut in butter with a pastry cutter or two knives.

In another bowl beat the egg yolks thoroughly and add the milk. Stir into the flour mixture.

In a clean bowl with clean beaters, beat the egg whites until they hold peaks. Gently fold them into the batter.

Spoon the batter into pans and bake for 30 minutes, until puffed and golden brown.

QUICK BREADS

BASIC

BROWN BREAD

¶ *Boston brown bread is one of this country's oldest breads.
A direct descendant of English steamed puddings, it was
made by the early settlers with a mixture of rye and
whole wheat flours. This recipe is a modification using
unbleached flour, whole wheat flour, and corn meal.
Save your coffee cans in anticipation!*

2 LOAVES

    1   cup unbleached flour, sifted
    ¾   teaspoon baking powder
    ¾   teaspoon salt
    1   cup whole wheat flour
    1   cup yellow stone-ground corn meal
    ¾   cup dark seedless raisins
    ¾   teaspoon baking soda
    1   tablespoon boiling water
  2¼   cups sour milk or buttermilk
    ¾   cup dark molasses
    2   eggs, slightly beaten

Grease two 1-pound coffee cans.

Sift together the flour, baking powder, and salt. Stir in
the whole wheat flour, corn meal, and raisins.

In a small dish or cup dissolve the baking soda in the
boiling water.

In a large bowl mix the sour milk with the molasses and stir in the baking soda mixture. Add the dry ingredients, stirring until well blended. Add beaten eggs to batter and stir thoroughly.

Pour batter into cans, filling them two-thirds full. Cover cans with aluminum foil and tie the foil securely with string. Place the cans upright on a rack in a large, deep kettle. Add enough boiling water to reach halfway up the sides of the cans. Place the kettle over low heat and cover. Steaming time will be approximately 2½ hours or until a cake tester inserted in center of bread comes out clean.

There is an alternative method of steaming. Steam for 2 hours over low heat as above and then remove cans from the kettle, remove foil, and allow cans to dry out in a slow oven (preheated at 300 degrees, for 15 minutes) for 10 to 15 minutes.

Remove cans from heat and allow to cool on a wire cake rack for 15 minutes. Remove bread from cans and serve warm or at room temperature.

CHOCOLATE BREAD

¶ *This is a real dessert bread and can be made with the melted chocolate on top or left plain. It freezes well but chances are that the bread will disappear too quickly to be frozen.*

1 LOAF

2 cups unbleached flour
2 teaspoons baking powder
½ teaspoon salt
2 eggs

⅔ cup granulated sugar
½ stick unsalted butter, melted
2 squares unsweetened chocolate, grated
½ cup hot orange juice
¼ cup hot water
1 teaspoon vanilla

TOPPING (Optional):
1½ square semi-sweet chocolate, grated
1 tablespoon granulated sugar

Preheat oven to 350 degrees. Grease an 8 × 4½ × 2½-inch loaf pan.

Sift together flour, baking powder, and salt. Set aside.

In another bowl beat the eggs, then add granulated sugar, and beat thoroughly. Add melted butter, unsweetened chocolate, hot orange juice, hot water, and vanilla. Stir until mixture is completely blended.

Add liquid mixture to dry ingredients and mix thoroughly, being careful not to beat or overmix.

Pour into baking pan and bake at 350 degrees for 40 to 45 minutes. A wooden pick inserted in center of bread should come out clean.

If chocolate topping is desired, sprinkle top of bread with grated chocolate mixed with sugar immediately after baking and put into oven for 2 to 3 minutes. Remove pan and spread topping evenly.

CINNAMON BREAD

¶ *This cinnamon bread should be served warm. It is a good breakfast bread or wonderful with a pot of hot tea in the afternoon.*

ABOUT 9 GOOD-SIZED PIECES

     4 tablespoons (½ stick) unsalted butter
    ⅔ cup brown sugar
     1 egg, beaten
    ½ cup milk
    1¾ cups unbleached flour, sifted
     1 tablespoon baking powder
    ¼ teaspoon salt

TOPPING:
     3 tablespoons brown sugar
    1½ teaspoons cinnamon

Preheat oven to 400 degrees. Grease an 8-inch square pan.

Cream butter, add sugar, and beat until thoroughly blended. Add egg and milk and stir until mixed thoroughly.

Sift the flour, baking powder, and salt into a bowl. Add liquid mixture and stir just until blended.

Spoon into greased pan. Top with the brown sugar and cinnamon mix together. Bake for 20 minutes and serve warm.

CORN BREAD

¶ *This recipe is based on a variation of an old Shaker bread that I discovered several years ago. It is best served warm.*

1 cup yellow stone-ground corn meal
1 cup unbleached flour, sifted
1 teaspoon salt
2 tablespoons granulated sugar
1 teaspoon baking soda
1 teaspoon cream of tartar
1 cup sour cream
¼ cup milk
1 egg, slightly beaten
1 tablespoon unsalted butter, melted

Preheat oven to 425 degrees. Grease an 8-inch square pan.

Sift together the corn meal, flour, salt, sugar, baking soda, and cream of tartar into a large bowl. Add the sour cream, milk, egg, and melted butter and stir thoroughly with a spoon. Do not overmix.

Turn into the greased pan and bake 20 minutes or until a tester comes out clean.

GRAHAM BREAD

¶ *Graham flour can frequently be substituted for whole wheat flour with no loss in nutrients. It contributes a different taste to the bread.*

1 LOAF

1½ cups unbleached flour, sifted
1 tablespoon baking powder
½ teaspoon salt
1 cup graham flour
¾ cup chopped pecans
1 cup milk
½ cup honey
1 egg, beaten
2 tablespoons unsalted butter, melted

Preheat oven to 350 degrees. Grease a 9 × 5 × 3-inch loaf pan.

Sift together into a large bowl the flour, baking powder, and salt. Add graham flour and pecans and stir in thoroughly.

In a separate bowl mix together the milk, honey, beaten egg, and melted butter. Stir the liquid ingredients into the dry mixture just until moistened.

Pour batter into pan and bake for 50 to 60 minutes or until a wooden pick inserted in center comes out clean. Cool for 10 minutes on a wire rack. Remove bread from pan and allow to cool thoroughly. Serve with a berry preserve or an orange marmalade.

OATMEAL-RAISIN BREAD

¶ *This is an easy, quick recipe and freezes extremely well.*

1 LOAF

1⅓ cups unbleached flour, sifted
1 tablespoon baking powder
½ teaspoon salt
½ teaspoon nutmeg
⅔ cup firmly packed dark brown sugar
1½ cups rolled oats
¾ cup raisins
1⅓ cups milk
1 egg, beaten
¼ cup (½ stick) unsalted butter, melted

Preheat oven to 350 degrees. Grease a 9 × 5 × 3-inch loaf pan.

Sift together flour, baking powder, salt, and nutmeg into a large bowl. Mix in brown sugar, rolled oats, and raisins.

Into the milk stir the beaten egg and melted butter. Add to the flour mixture. Stir just until blended.

Spoon into loaf pan and bake for 50 to 55 minutes or until bread shrinks from sides of pan. Cool for 5 minutes, remove from pan, and allow to cool thoroughly.

SPOON BREAD

ONE 8-INCH SPOON BREAD

2 cups milk
1 cup yellow stone-ground corn meal
1 teaspoon salt
1 egg, beaten
2 tablespoons unsalted butter, melted
1 teaspoon baking powder
1 teaspoon granulated sugar

Preheat oven to 425 degrees. Grease one 8-inch-square cake pan or one 8-inch-round cast iron pan.

Bring milk to a boil in a large, heavy saucepan. Carefully stir in corn meal. Add salt and cook for 2 to 3 minutes. Remove from heat. Stir in beaten egg, butter, baking powder, and sugar.

Pour batter into greased pan and bake for 20 minutes, until golden and crusty. This bread is best served warm, straight from the pan.

SWOOP BREAD

¶ *My friend Lisa Ross-Miller is an artist whose creativity in the kitchen I have always admired. She shared this recipe with me and we are both fond of it for two reasons. It always brings compliments, and it is a very simple bread to make.*

2 LOAVES

4 cups whole wheat flour
1 cup granulated sugar
1 teaspoon salt
1 quart (4 cups) buttermilk
4 teaspoons baking soda

Preheat oven to 375 degrees. Grease two 8½ × 4½ × 2½-inch glass pans.

Combine the whole wheat flour, sugar, and salt. Add the buttermilk and baking soda and mix well.

Pour into the pans. Reduce oven temperature to 350 degrees and bake for 1 hour, until a tester comes out clean. Bread should be a very rich, dark brown color.

Cool for 10 minutes on a wire rack, and remove from pan. This is delicious served warm or cool.

FRUITS

APPLESAUCE BREAD

¶ *Freshly made applesauce is the basis of this bread.*

1 Loaf

- ½ cup vegetable oil
- ¾ cup honey
- 1 cup fresh applesauce
- ¾ cup unbleached flour, sifted
- 1 teaspoon baking soda
- 1 teaspoon cinnamon
- ¼ teaspoon ground cloves
- ½ cup whole wheat flour
- ¼ cup bran, preferably unprocessed
- ¾ cup raisins

Preheat oven to 350 degrees. Grease a 9 × 5 × 3-inch loaf pan.

Blend the oil and honey in a large bowl and beat until smooth. Mix in the applesauce thoroughly.

Sift together into a bowl the unbleached flour, baking soda, cinnamon, and ground cloves. Mix in the whole wheat flour and the bran.

Add the dry ingredients to the oil/honey mixture and stir until thoroughly blended. Fold in raisins.

Spoon into greased pan and bake at 350 degrees for 40

to 50 minutes or until top of bread springs back when touched lightly in center. Cool on a wire rack for 10 minutes. Remove from pan and cool thoroughly.

NOTE: Fresh applesauce can be made by peeling, coring and cutting apples into small chunks. Cook with a small amount of water over a low heat until apples are soft. Turn off heat and let apples remain in pot for ten minutes. All water should be absorbed.

Apples may be put through a sieve or used in soft chunky manner. About two cups raw apples will boil down to one cup. This may vary. If cooking apples for baking purposes, I don't add any spices. When cooking applesauce for use with a meal, I often add a little cinnamon and one of the following—nutmeg, cloves or allspice. Nuts and raisins can be added after the cooking.

APRICOT BRAN BREAD

¶ *The juices in this recipe bring out the taste of the apricot and make a good balance to the bran. This bread should always be made 24 hours before using.*

1 LOAF

1½ cups dried apricot halves
¾ cup orange juice
¼ cup pineapple juice
2 cups unbleached flour, sifted
1 tablespoon baking powder
½ teaspoon baking soda
½ teaspoon salt

¼ cup (½ stick) unsalted butter
½ cup honey
1 egg, beaten
½ cup milk
1 cup bran
2 teaspoons grated orange peel
½ cup slivered almonds or chopped filberts (optional)

Prepare the apricots: Using scissors, snip the dried apricots into ¼- to ½-inch pieces and place in a small saucepan over moderately low heat with the juices. Heat until mixture just barely comes to a boil, lower heat, and simmer for 5 minutes. Remove from heat and cool.

Preheat oven to 325 degrees. Grease a 9 × 5 × 3-inch loaf pan.

Sift together flour, baking powder, baking soda, and salt.

In a large bowl cream the butter and honey until blended. Add egg and milk and mix well. Stir in the bran, grated orange peel, the apricots and juices, and nuts (if you use them) into the butter mixture, mixing well. Add the dry ingredients and mix only until the batter is moistened thoroughly.

Pour into loaf pan and bake for 55 to 60 minutes, or until a wooden pick inserted in center comes out clean. Cool bread on a wire rack for 10 minutes and then remove from pan and cool completely. Wrap bread in foil and store 24 hours before slicing.

BLUEBERRY-ORANGE BREAD

¶ *Blueberry and orange is one of my favorite combinations. By all means use fresh blueberries, and if you take a minute to squeeze fresh orange juice the bread will benefit. The topping is optional, or it can be varied to suit you.*

1 LOAF

2½ cups unbleached flour, sifted
1 tablespoon baking powder
½ teaspoon baking soda
½ cup granulated sugar
½ teaspoon salt
1 cup fresh blueberries, washed, drained, and tossed in ¼ cup flour
3 eggs
½ cup milk
½ cup (1 stick) unsalted butter, melted
1½ tablespoons grated orange rind
⅓ cup orange juice, preferably freshly squeezed

TOPPING:
¼ cup orange juice
3 tablespoons granulated sugar

Preheat oven to 350 degrees. Grease a 9 × 5 × 3-inch loaf pan.

Sift together into a large bowl the flour, baking powder, baking soda, sugar, and salt. Toss the blueberries with the ¼ cup flour and add to the mixture. Stir gently to mix in blueberries thoroughly.

In a separate bowl, beat the eggs. Add milk, melted butter, grated orange rind, and orange juice. Pour the liquid into the dry ingredients and stir until the flour is moistened. Do not overmix.

Spoon into pan and bake for 1 hour or until a wooden pick inserted in the center comes out clean.

Immediately after bread comes out of the oven, stir the

topping ingredients together and spoon across the top of the warm bread. Allow bread to cool 10 minutes in pan on a wire rack. Remove from pan and cool thoroughly.

VARIATIONS:
Other seasonal berries such as blackberries or raspberries may be substituted for the blueberries.

KIWI BREAD

¶ *The kiwi has a mild, almost grapelike taste when baked in this bread. Since it is so low-keyed I have not included any spices or nuts.*

1 LOAF

2 cups unbleached flour, sifted
1 teaspoon baking powder
¼ teaspoon baking soda
½ teaspoon salt
½ cup (1 stick) unsalted butter
⅔ cup granulated sugar
2 eggs
1 cup peeled, mashed kiwi fruit (about 3 or 4 kiwis)

Preheat oven to 350 degrees. Grease and flour a 9 × 5 × 3-inch loaf pan.

Sift together the flour, baking powder, baking soda, and salt.

In a large bowl cream the butter, add the sugar gradually, and beat until light and fluffy. Add eggs, one at a time, to the creamed mixture, beating well after each one. Stir in the kiwis. Fold in the dry ingredients gently, stirring only until batter is completely moistened.

Spoon batter into pan and bake for 60 to 70 minutes or

until a wooden pick inserted in center comes out clean. Cool for 10 minutes on a wire rack and then remove from pan and cool completely.

❦

LEMON BREAD

¶ *This bread has inspired more debate than any other I have baked. For some it is too tart and others argue it is just right. The main ingredient list will make a moderately mild version, with substitutions in parenthesis for a very tart bread. It is really the baker's decision. If you find it too lemony by all means adjust the lemon juice and sugar. Use nothing but freshly squeezed lemon juice. And it is absolutely essential that this bread be baked the day before you plan to serve it.*

1 LOAF

½ cup (1 stick) unsalted butter, softened
⅔ cup granulated sugar (or ½ cup)
2 eggs
1½ cups sifted unbleached flour
1 teaspoon baking powder
½ teaspoon salt
½ cup milk
3 tablespoons lemon juice
1½ tablespoons grated lemon rind

GLAZE:
¼ cup granulated sugar
¼ cup lemon juice (or ⅓ cup)

Preheat oven to 325 degrees. Grease a 9 × 5 × 3-inch loaf pan.

Cream butter and sugar in a large bowl. Beat in eggs, one at a time.

Sift together flour, baking powder, and salt. Add dry ingredients to creamed mixture alternately with milk. Mix well. Stir in lemon juice and rind by hand.

Bake for 60 to 70 minutes or until a light, golden brown and cake springs back to a light touch. As soon as you remove the bread from the oven, stir together the glaze ingredients. Pierce the top of the bread with a wooden pick in several places (primarily towards the center) and pour on the glaze while the bread is still warm.

Allow bread to cool in pan. After bread is thoroughly cooled, remove from pan, wrap in plastic or foil, and do not slice for 24 hours. This bread is best sliced thin.

PLUM BREAD

¶ *This recipe calls for fresh Italian plums, but other types may be substituted as long as they are ripe.*

1 LOAF

2 cups unbleached flour, sifted
1 teaspoon baking powder
½ teaspoon salt
½ cup granulated sugar
4 tablespoons (½ stick) unsalted butter
½ cup milk
1 egg, beaten

TOPPING:
¼ cup light brown sugar
1 teaspoon cinnamon
1 egg, well beaten
  Fresh Italian plums, halved and pitted (about 8 to 12 depending upon size)

Preheat oven to 350 degrees. Grease a 9 × 5 × 3-inch loaf pan.

Sift together into a large bowl flour, baking powder, salt, and sugar. Add butter and work in with a pastry blender, two knives, or your fingers until mixture looks like coarse meal. Add milk and egg and stir just enough to dampen dry ingredients.

Spread this batter in the bottom of the loaf pan. Arrange halved plums, skin side down, over the batter. Mix the brown sugar and cinnamon and sprinkle over top. Then drizzle beaten egg on top.

Bake for 1 hour. Allow bread to cool 10 minutes in pan. Remove and cool thoroughly.

STRAWBERRY BREAD

1 Loaf

1 ½ cups unbleached flour
 ½ teaspoon baking soda
 ½ teaspoon salt
 1 teaspoon cinnamon
 2 eggs
 ⅔ cup packed light brown sugar
 ½ cup vegetable oil
 1 heaping cup chopped fresh strawberries

Preheat oven to 350 degrees. Grease a 9 × 5 × 3-inch loaf pan.

Sift flour. Then sift again with the baking soda, salt, and cinnamon. Set aside.

Beat eggs in a large bowl until light. Add sugar and oil and stir just until mixed. Do not beat or overmix. Add strawberries and mix. Fold in dry ingredients and stir thoroughly.

Pour into greased pan and bake for 1 hour or until a wooden pick inserted into center comes out clean. Cool for 10 minutes on a rack. Remove from pan and cool completely.

FRUITS AND NUTS

ALMOND-LIME LOAF

¶ *This unique fruit-nut loaf is best made a day ahead to allow these delicate flavors to mellow. Serve it in thin slices. It toasts nicely.*

1 LOAF

  3 cups minus 2 tablespoons sifted unbleached flour
 ¾ cup granulated sugar
  1 tablespoon baking powder
  1 teaspoon salt
 ¼ teaspoon baking soda
 ¼ teaspoon mace
  3 ounces sliced unblanched almonds
  1 tablespoon grated lime rind
  1 egg
  1 cup milk
  5 tablespoons unsalted butter, melted
  2 tablespoons lime juice

TOPPING:
  2 tablespoons granulated sugar
  1 tablespoon lime juice
  1 tablespoon grated lime rind

Preheat oven to 350 degrees. Grease a 9 × 5 × 3-inch loaf pan.

Sift and measure flour. Add ¾ cup sugar, baking powder, salt, baking soda, and mace and sift twice more into a large bowl. Stir in the almonds and 1 tablespoon lime rind.

Beat egg well with milk in a small bowl. Stir in the melted butter and 2 tablespoons lime juice. Add this mixture all at once to the flour mixture and stir just until evenly moist.

Spoon into prepared pan and bake for 60 to 70 minutes, or until a wooden pick inserted in center comes out clean.

Immediately after removing bread from oven, combine the topping ingredients in a small bowl and spoon evenly over warm bread.

Cool in pan for 10 minutes. Loosen around edges with a knife and turn out onto a wire rack. Cool completely. Wrap loaf in foil or wax paper. Store overnight before slicing.

FRESH APPLE BREAD

¶ *Apples are a wonderful addition to any meal and are so plentiful in the fall and winter that you really should take advantage of them. This bread can be baked early in the day and would be delicious served with a dinner featuring a pork main dish.*

1 LOAF

2	cups unbleached flour
2	teaspoons baking powder
¾	teaspoon cinnamon
½	cup (1 stick) unsalted butter
⅔	cup granulated sugar
2	eggs
1½	cups peeled, finely grated apples
½	cup chopped walnuts or pecans

Preheat oven to 350 degrees. Grease a 9 × 5 × 3-inch loaf pan.

Sift flour into a bowl. Sift again with baking powder and salt. Then add the cinnamon. Set aside.

Cream the butter and sugar together in a large bowl until light and fluffy. Beat in the eggs, one at a time, beating well after each addition. Stir in the dry ingredients and the grated apples alternately. Fold in nuts.

Pour into the loaf pan and bake for 1 hour or until a wooden pick inserted in center comes out clean.

Cool in pan on a rack for 10 minutes. Turn out of pan and cool completely before slicing.

APPLE-DATE LOAF

¶ *This makes a rich bread that keeps well if wrapped tightly. It can be kept several days in the refrigerator.*

1 LOAF

2¼ cups unbleached flour, sifted
2 teaspoons baking powder
1 teaspoon baking soda
¾ teaspoon ground cinnamon
¼ teaspoon ground nutmeg
1 teaspoon salt
½ cup (1 stick) unsalted butter
½ cup granulated sugar
1 egg
1 cup milk
1 cup peeled, cored, and coarsely chopped apples
½ cup coarsely chopped pitted dates
¾ cup chopped walnuts

Preheat oven to 350 degrees. Grease a 9 × 5 × 3-inch loaf pan.

Sift together twice flour, baking powder, baking soda, cinnamon, nutmeg, and salt.

In a large bowl cream butter and sugar together until fluffy. Add egg and beat until well blended. Add flour mixture to butter mixture alternately with milk, blending well after each addition. Stir apples, dates, and walnuts into batter.

Pour batter into pan and bake for 65 to 70 minutes, or until a wooden pick inserted in center of the bread comes out clean.

Cool bread on a wire rack for 10 minutes. Remove from pan and cool completely. When cool, wrap bread tightly in foil and store overnight before slicing.

BANANA-DATE BREAD

¶ *This version of popular banana bread keeps well for several days wrapped in foil in the refrigerator. Toast lightly and spread with one of the honey butters on page 128.*

1 LOAF

2 cups unbleached flour, sifted
1 tablespoon baking powder
½ teaspoon salt
½ teaspoon grated nutmeg
½ cup (1 stick) unsalted butter
½ cup granulated sugar
1 egg
¾ cup milk
1 cup mashed ripe banana
1 teaspoon vanilla
⅓ cup pitted and chopped dates
½ cup chopped walnuts

Preheat oven to 350 degrees. Grease a 9 × 5 × 3-inch loaf pan.

Sift together onto wax paper the flour, baking powder, salt, and nutmeg.

In a large bowl cream butter and sugar until light and fluffy. Add the egg and beat thoroughly. Add milk. Stir in the dry ingredients. Add the mashed banana and vanilla. Fold in the dates and nuts and mix well.

Spoon batter into pan and bake for 1 hour or until a wooden pick inserted in center comes out clean. Cool for 10 minutes, remove from pan, and cool completely on wire rack.

BANANA-PISTACHIO BREAD

¶ *The first quick bread I remember baking with my mother when I was a child was banana bread. I was fascinated that we could make a bread without waiting for it to rise and without kneading, and I was always delighted when some overripe bananas would prompt my mother to decide we would make banana bread. This is my version with pistachios, but walnuts are just as suitable.*

1 LOAF

2 cups sifted unbleached flour
1 teaspoon baking powder
½ teaspoon baking soda
½ teaspoon salt
⅔ cup granulated sugar
⅓ cup softened unsalted butter
2 eggs
3 tablespoons sour milk
1 cup mashed very ripe bananas (about 2 large ones)
½ cup chopped pistachio nuts

Preheat oven to 350 degrees. Grease a 9 × 5 × 3-inch loaf pan.

Sift together flour, baking powder, baking soda, and salt.

In a large bowl cream the sugar and butter. Beat in one egg at a time. Stir in sour milk and banana into creamed mixture.

Mix dry ingredients into the liquid/creamed mixture until all the flour is moistened. Fold in nuts.

Pour into loaf pan and allow to stand at room temperature for 20 minutes.

Bake banana bread at 350 degrees for 45 to 55 minutes. Allow to cool 10 minutes in pan. Remove and cool thoroughly on a rack.

CHERRY BREAD 1

¶ *The cream cheese here is a departure from the usual cherry bread recipe. If fresh cherries are unavailable a 16-ounce package of* tart *frozen cherries, thawed and drained, may be substituted.*

1 Loaf

- 1 3-ounce package cream cheese, softened
- 2 tablespoons granulated sugar
- 1 tablespoon flour
- 1 egg yolk
- 2 cups unbleached flour
- ½ cup firmly packed light brown sugar
- 1 tablespoon grated orange peel
- 1½ teaspoons baking powder
- ½ teaspoon salt
- ¼ cup (½ stick) unsalted butter
- ½ cup freshly squeezed orange juice
- 1 egg, slightly beaten
- 2 cups pitted fresh tart cherries

Preheat oven to 350 degrees. Grease a 9 × 5 × 3-inch loaf pan.

Beat cream cheese, 2 tablespoons sugar, 1 tablespoon flour, and the egg yolk in a small bowl until smooth. Set aside.

Sift the flour onto wax paper. Then combine the flour, brown sugar, orange peel, baking powder, and salt in a large bowl. Cut in the butter as for pastry until the mixture resembles coarse crumbs. Stir in the orange juice and the egg until the flour mixture is moistened. Fold in cherries.

Spoon two-thirds of the cherry batter into the greased loaf pan. Pour the cream cheese mixture evenly over batter. Spoon remaining batter on top and bake for 75 to 90 minutes or until a wooden pick inserted in center comes out clean. Cool in pan for 10 minutes. Remove from pan and cool completely on wire rack.

CHERRY NUT BREAD 2

¶ *Almonds and cherries seem to have a natural affinity, but you could substitute pecans, walnuts, or another nut. If fresh cherries are not available, frozen or canned fruit may be used, although my preference is to take advantage of seasonal produce at its peak. (If canned cherries are used, rinse in cold water to remove the sugary syrup.)*

1 LOAF

½ cup orange juice
1 cup pitted sweet cherries
¼ cup (½ stick) unsalted butter, softened
2 eggs
½ cup granulated sugar
2 teaspoons grated lemon rind
1½ cups unbleached flour, sifted
½ teaspoon baking soda
½ teaspoon baking powder
½ teaspoon salt
½ cup chopped almonds

Preheat oven to 350 degrees. Grease an 8½ × 4½ × 3-inch loaf pan.

In a small saucepan bring the orange juice to a simmer.

In a large bowl combine cherries, softened butter, and hot orange juice and stir the mixture until the butter is melted.

In a separate bowl beat the eggs until they are light and lemon colored. Add the sugar and grated lemon rind and beat the mixture until it forms a ribbon when the beaters are lifted. Add the egg mixture to the cherry mixture.

Sift together onto wax paper the flour, baking soda, baking powder, and salt. Fold the flour mixture into the cherry mixture and stir until it is combined. Fold in the nuts.

Pour into the greased pan and bake for 1 hour or until a wooden pick inserted in the center comes out clean. Cool the bread in the pan for 10 minutes on a rack. Remove from pan and allow to cool thoroughly. Serve with a lemon butter or a plain cheese or cream cheese, if you wish.

CRANBERRY-ORANGE PECAN BREAD

¶ *The combination of cranberries and orange is one I have used in a variety of recipes. The sweetness of the orange balances well with the tang of the cranberries, and requires a minimum of sugar. This bread is excellent just sliced from the loaf but is also excellent with a mild cheese. It can be sliced thin and toasted slightly in a toaster-oven.*

1 Loaf

    1   cup unbleached flour, sifted
    ½   cup granulated sugar
    1½ teaspoons baking powder
    ½   teaspoon salt
    ½   teaspoon baking soda
    ¼   teaspoon cinnamon
    ¼   teaspoon ground cloves
    1   cup whole wheat flour
        Grated rind of 1 orange (about 1½ tablespoons)
    ¾   cup orange juice, preferably freshly squeezed
    1   large egg
    ¼   cup (½ stick) unsalted butter, melted
    1   cup fresh cranberries
    ½   cup chopped pecans

Preheat oven to 350 degrees. Grease a 9 × 5 × 3-inch loaf pan.

Sift together the unbleached flour, sugar, baking powder, salt, baking soda, cinnamon, and cloves into a large bowl. Stir in the whole wheat flour.

Whisk together lightly the orange rind, orange juice, egg, and melted butter and mix the wet ingredients into the dry ingredients until just blended. Do not overmix. Fold the cranberries and pecans into the batter.

Pour batter into greased pan and bake for 1 hour or until a wooden pick inserted in center comes out clean.

Cool on a rack. Remove from pan after 10 minutes and cool thoroughly. Wrap in foil or plastic wrap for storage.

CRANBERRY NUT BREAD

¶ *Cranberries are associated with the winter holidays such as Thanksgiving and Christmas but are a zestful addition to meals all during the fall and winter. This bread is best baked the day before serving.*

1 LOAF

2 cups unbleached flour
¾ cup granulated sugar
1½ teaspoons baking powder
½ teaspoon baking soda
½ teaspoon salt
¼ cup (½ stick) unsalted butter
1 egg
¾ cup orange juice, preferably freshly squeezed
1 tablespoon grated orange rind
1½ cups chopped fresh cranberries
½ cup chopped walnuts

Preheat oven to 350 degrees. Grease a 9 × 5 × 3-inch loaf pan.

Sift flour. Sift again with sugar, baking powder, baking soda, and salt into a large bowl. Cut in butter until the mixture resembles coarse meal. This can be done with two knives, a pastry cutter, or by hand.

Beat the egg until it is light in color and thick. Stir in orange juice and rind. Lightly stir this mixture into the flour mixture just until the ingredients are blended. Do not overmix. Fold in cranberries and nuts.

Pour batter into prepared pan and bake for approximately 75 minutes until it is golden brown. It should spring back when lightly touched. Cool on a rack and remove from pan after 10 minutes. After bread is thoroughly cooled, wrap it in foil and keep overnight before slicing.

DATE NUT BREAD

¶ *Here is a basic traditional recipe for the perennial fa-*
vorite. Substitutions or additions can be made to your
whim. It makes fine sandwiches when sliced thin and
spread with fresh cream cheese.

1 LOAF

　1　cup boiling water
　¾　cup pitted and chopped dates
　¼　cup orange juice
1½　cups unbleached flour, sifted
　1　teaspoon baking soda
　½　teaspoon salt
　¼　teaspoon ground mace
　¼　cup (½ stick) unsalted butter
　½　cup firmly packed brown sugar
　1　egg
　1　cup chopped walnuts
　1　tablespoon grated orange rind

Pour boiling water over dates in a large bowl. Stir in orange
juice and allow to stand while preparing batter.

Heat oven to 325 degrees. Grease a 9 × 5 × 3-inch loaf
pan. Dust with flour.

Sift together onto wax paper the flour, baking soda, salt,
and mace.

In a large bowl cream butter and sugar until well blended.
Add the egg and beat well. Stir the date mixture and mix
into the creamed ingredients. Blend thoroughly. Add the
flour mixture and stir only until completely moistened.
Fold in nuts and orange peel.

Pour batter into pan and bake for 65 to 70 minutes or
until a wooden pick inserted in center comes out clean.
Cool for 10 minutes and then remove from pan and cool
completely on a wire rack.

❦

HONEY-PRUNE BREAD

1¾ cups unbleached flour
1½ teaspoons baking powder
 ½ teaspoon salt
 ½ teaspoon baking soda
 2 tablespoons unsalted butter
 ⅓ cup mild honey, such as clover
 2 eggs
 ½ cup sour milk
 ½ cup chopped prunes, softened in hot water
 ½ cup chopped pecans
 ½ teaspoon grated lemon rind

Preheat oven to 350 degrees. Grease an 8½ × 4½ × 2½-inch loaf pan.

Sift flour. Then sift together flour, baking powder, salt, and baking soda.

Cream together in a large bowl the butter and honey. Add eggs, one at time, beating well after each addition. Add dry ingredients and sour milk alternately to the creamed mixture. Beat until well blended. Stir in prunes, pecans, and lemon rind.

Pour batter into pan and bake for 60 to 70 minutes. Allow to cool for 10 minutes before removing from pan.

ORANGE-OATMEAL BREAD

¶ *This is another of my mother's recipes. I think she developed many recipes with oatmeal because her children refused to eat the traditional breakfast food in its ordinary form. This is certainly a much more delicious way to enjoy oatmeal.*

1 LOAF

    2 teaspoons granulated sugar
    1 orange, peeled and cut into very small pieces (about
       1 cup)
1½ cups sifted, unbleached flour
    ½ teaspoon salt
4½ teaspoons baking powder
    ¼ teaspoon soda
    ½ cup granulated sugar
    1 cup oatmeal
    2 tablespoons unsalted butter, melted
    2 eggs beaten
    ⅔ cup water
    2 tablespoons grated orange peel

Preheat oven to 350 degrees. Grease a 9 × 5 × 3-inch loaf pan.

Sprinkle 2 teaspoons sugar over orange. Set aside. Sift flour, salt, baking powder, baking soda, and ¾ cup sugar together. Stir in oats.

Combine melted butter, eggs, water, orange peel, and orange in a separate bowl. Blend well.

Add liquid to the dry ingredients and stir just until blended.

Pour into baking pan and bake 50 to 55 minutes until a wooden pick comes out clean.

Cool for 10 minutes in the pan. Remove from pan, cool thoroughly on a rack.

ORANGE-DATE BREAD

¶ *This bread can be made any time of the year but is especially welcome when other fruits such as berries are out of season. It is good served plain or with cream cheese.*

1 LOAF

1   medium-sized orange
    Boiling water
⅔ cup finely chopped pitted dates
2   tablespoons unsalted butter, melted
1   teaspoon vanilla
1   egg, well beaten
2   cups unbleached flour, sifted
¼ teaspoon salt
1   teaspoon baking powder
½ teaspoon baking soda
⅔ cup granulated sugar
½ cup chopped almonds

Preheat oven to 350 degrees. Grease and flour a 9 × 5 × 3-inch loaf pan.

Squeeze orange into measuring cup, add orange pulp (no seeds, pith, or rind), and add boiling water to make 1 cup. Pour into mixing bowl.

Grate the orange, making sure not to include the white pulp of the orange. Add grated orange rind and dates to orange juice/water. Blend in melted butter, vanilla, and egg.

Sift flour, salt, baking powder, baking soda, and sugar together. Blend dry ingredients into the liquid mixture. Fold in nuts.

Pour batter into pan and bake for 60 to 70 minutes or until a wooden pick inserted in center of bread comes out clean. Cool bread on a rack for 10 minutes. Remove from pan and cool thoroughly.

❦

PECAN-RAISIN BREAD

¶ *This is based on a Greek recipe that was baked frequently in my mother's kitchen. The recipe can easily be doubled and baked in a 13 × 9 × 2-inch pan. Some prefer this bread with confectioner's sugar sprinkled on top but I happen to like it just as it is.*

1 LOAF

- 2 cups unbleached flour
- 2½ teaspoons baking powder
- ½ teaspoon ground cinnamon
- ¼ teaspoon ground cloves
- ¼ teaspoon salt
- ½ cup (1 stick) unsalted butter
- ½ cup granulated sugar
- 2 eggs
- ¾ cup milk
- ½ cup light sultana raisins
- ½ cup chopped pecans

Preheat oven to 350 degrees. Grease a 9 × 5 × 3-inch loaf pan.

Sift flour. Then sift together flour, baking powder, cinnamon, cloves, and salt into a bowl. Set aside.

Cream butter and sugar until light and fluffy. Add eggs, one at a time, beating after each.

Add dry ingredients to batter alternately with milk, beating quickly each time. Fold in raisins and pecans.

Spoon into prepared pan and bake for 60 to 75 minutes or until a wooden pick inserted in center comes out clean. Bread must be baked thoroughly or it crumbles when cut. Cool on rack for 10 minutes. Remove from pan and allow to cool thoroughly before cutting. This bread is especially good served with a freshly brewed cup of coffee. It will keep nicely for 24 hours if wrapped in foil.

PINEAPPLE-COCONUT BREAD

¶ *Just the name of this bread makes one think of a summer day or a holiday in the Caribbean. I prefer to toast the coconut but you may use it plain.*

1 LOAF

3 cups minus 2 tablespoons unbleached flour, sifted
1 tablespoon baking powder
¾ teaspoon baking soda
¾ teaspoon salt
3 eggs
½ cup vegetable oil
½ cup mild honey, such as clover
1 cup undrained crushed pineapple, canned
½ cup flaked coconut, toasted if you like
½ cup water
¾ cup chopped Brazil nuts

Preheat oven to 350 degrees. Grease a 9 × 5 × 3-inch loaf pan.

Sift together in a large bowl the flour, baking powder, baking soda, and salt.

In a separate bowl beat the eggs until thick and lemon-colored.

Combine the oil, honey, undrained pineapple, coconut, and water, add to the eggs, and mix well. Mix this liquid combination with the dry ingredients stirring only until blended thoroughly. Fold in the nuts.

Spoon batter into baking pan and bake for 1 hour at 350 degrees. Reduce heat to 325 degrees and bake 15 minutes longer or until a wooden pick inserted in the center comes out clean. Allow to cool 10 minutes in pan. Then remove from pan and cool completely on a wire rack.

This bread can be made 24 hours before serving. Cool and wrap in foil or plastic wrap. Serve with cream cheese.

RHUBARB BREAD

¶ *Rhubarb can be used in place of gooseberries, apples, or plums. It is probably most widely known for its use in pies, but why not branch out and try this bread. Be careful to use only the rhubarb stalks; the leaves are toxic. Rhubarb should be used as soon as possible after picking or purchasing.*

1 LOAF

¾ cup firmly packed light brown sugar
⅓ cup vegetable oil
1 egg, slightly beaten
½ cup sour milk or buttermilk
½ teaspoon baking soda
½ teaspoon vanilla
¼ teaspoon salt
1¼ cups unbleached flour, sifted
¾ cup chopped raw rhubarb, stalks only
¼ cup chopped walnuts
1½ tablespoons grated lemon peel

Preheat oven to 325 degrees. Grease an 8½ × 4½ × 2½-inch loaf pan.

In a large bowl combine the brown sugar, vegetable oil, and beaten egg. Mix until blended.

In a smaller bowl combine the sour milk, baking soda, vanilla, and salt.

Alternately add the milk mixture and the sifted flour to the brown sugar mixture, beating well after each addition. Fold in the rhubarb and walnuts.

Pour the batter into the prepared pan and bake for 45 to 55 minutes or until a wooden pick inserted in the center comes out clean. Cool on rack for 10 minutes. Remove from pan and cool completely.

SPIRITED FRUIT BREAD

¶ *This bread and its variations include liqueurs that com-
plement the nuts and fruits. Be sure to begin by mixing
the liqueur with the fruits so that the flavors will be absorbed while you prepare the batter.*

1 LOAF

1 cup chopped pitted dates
½ cup coffee liqueur such as Kahlúa
½ cup warm water
1 teaspoon grated orange peel
⅔ cup firmly packed dark brown sugar
2 tablespoons unsalted butter
1 egg
2 cups unbleached flour, sifted
1 teaspoon baking soda
½ teaspoon salt
⅔ cup chopped pecans

Combine dates, liqueur, water, and orange peel. Set aside
while preparing batter. Grease a 9 × 5 × 3-inch loaf pan.
Preheat oven to 350 degrees.

Cream together sugar, butter, and egg until fluffy.
Sift together the flour, baking soda, and salt. Add the
flour mixture to the creamed ingredients alternately with
the date mixture. Fold in pecans.
Spoon bread into loaf pan. Allow batter to stand 7 minutes and then bake in lower part of oven for 60 to 70
minutes. Cool on wire rack for 10 minutes and then remove from pan and allow to cool completely.

VARIATIONS:
Instead of Kahlúa, try almond liqueur (amaretto). For an
apricot-amaretto bread substitute apricots for the dates,
almonds for the pecans, and amaretto for the Kahlúa. For
a *rum-raisin* variation substitute raisins for the dates,
walnuts or filberts for the pecans, and ¼ cup rum for the
coffee liqueur.

NUTS AND SEEDS

MAPLE WALNUT BREAD

¶ *Try this bread on a wintry Sunday afternoon with a strong, hot cup of coffee and a new book to start reading.*

1 LOAF

- 2 cups unbleached flour
- 1 tablespoon baking powder
- 1 teaspoon salt
- 1 teaspoon powdered instant coffee
- ½ cup packed light brown sugar
- 1 egg, beaten
- 1 cup milk
- 1 tablespoon maple syrup
- ¼ cup (½ stick) unsalted butter, melted
- 1¼ cups coarsely chopped walnuts

Preheat oven to 350 degrees. Grease a 9 × 5 × 3-inch loaf pan.

Sift flour. Sift again with baking powder and salt into a large bowl. Stir in instant coffee and brown sugar.

In a separate bowl beat egg. Add milk, maple syrup, and melted butter. Stir until blended. Add liquid ingredients to dry ingredients and mix well. Fold in walnuts.

Bake for 60 to 65 minutes or until wooden pick inserted in center comes out clean. Let bread cool on rack for 15 minutes, then remove from pan and cool thoroughly. Wrap in foil or plastic wrap and store at room temperature for 24 hours before slicing.

❧

NUT LOAF

¶ *This is a "plain" nut bread that is anything but plain. It can be made with a variety of nuts instead of the walnuts included below. Just be sure to use ½ cup ground nuts and ½ cup chopped nuts (the same kind). This bread must be completely cooled before slicing and is best made 24 hours before using. It is especially good with fresh fruit.*

1 LOAF

3   cups unbleached flour, sifted
½   teaspoon salt
⅔   cup granulated sugar
1   tablespoon baking powder
1   egg
1   cup light cream
3   tablespoons unsalted butter, melted
½   cup ground walnuts
½   cup chopped walnuts

Preheat oven to 300 degrees. Grease a 9 × 5 × 3-inch loaf pan.

Sift together into a large bowl the flour, salt, sugar, and baking powder.

In another bowl beat the egg with the cream. Add to the flour mixture. Mix in the melted butter and the ground walnuts. Blend thoroughly. Fold in the chopped nuts.

Spoon into the loaf pan and allow to stand for 30 min-

• 101 •

utes before baking. Bake for 65 to 80 minutes until a wooden pick inserted in center comes out clean. Cool bread in pan for 10 minutes. Then turn out on a wire rack to cool completely.

❦

PEANUT BUTTER BREAD 1

¶ *Peanut butter is a healthy alternative to many commercial snacks and this bread is especially popular because it uses both peanuts and peanut butter.*

2 LOAVES

- 3 cups unbleached flour, sifted
- ½ teaspoon baking soda
- 1 teaspoon baking powder
- ½ teaspoon salt
- ½ teaspoon nutmeg
- 1 teaspoon allspice
- 3 eggs, beaten
- 1 cup brown sugar
- ¾ cup vegetable oil
- ½ cup crunchy peanut butter
- 1 cup mashed pumpkin or squash (canned or frozen may be used if fresh is unavailable)
- ½ cup chopped roasted unsalted peanuts

Preheat oven to 350 degrees. Grease and flour two 8½ × 4½ × 2½-inch loaf pans.

Sift into a bowl the flour, baking soda, baking powder, salt, nutmeg, and allspice together.

In a separate bowl combine beaten eggs with brown sugar, vegetable oil, and peanut butter. Beat until well blended. Add pumpkin and stir until completely mixed. Add dry ingredients and stir until well blended. Fold in peanuts.

Spoon batter into loaf pans and bake 65 to 75 minutes or until brown and resilient to the touch. Cool on wire rack for 10 minutes, remove from pan, and cool completely.

PEANUT BUTTER BREAD 2

¶ *The honey-nut spread on page 130 goes very well with this bread.*

1 LOAF

1¾ cups unbleached flour, sifted
1 teaspoon baking soda
½ teaspoon salt
⅔ cup packed dark brown sugar
⅓ cup creamy peanut butter
1 egg, well beaten
1 cup buttermilk
1 cup crushed peanuts

Preheat oven to 350 degrees. Grease a 9 × 5 × 3-inch loaf pan.

Sift together the flour, baking soda, and salt.
In a large bowl mix the brown sugar with the peanut butter. Stir in the beaten egg and beat until smooth. Add the flour mixture and buttermilk alternately to the peanut butter mixture, mixing until smooth after each addition. Fold in crushed peanuts.
Pour into greased loaf pan and bake for 1 hour until lightly browned. Cool for 10 minutes on a wire rack, remove from pan, and cool completely.

TAHINI (SESAME) BREAD

¶ *"Tahinopita," as this is called in Greek, is frequently made during Lent when no dairy products are consumed. It is a nutritious and simple bread to make anytime.*

1 LARGE LOAF

- 3 cups unbleached flour, sifted
- 1 tablespoon baking powder
- ¾ teaspoon salt
- 1 teaspoon baking soda
- ⅔ cup granulated sugar
- ½ cup walnuts
- ½ cup sultana raisins
- 1½ tablespoons grated orange peel
- 1 cup orange juice
- ½ cup water
- 1 cup tahini (sesame paste), available in ethnic markets and many supermarkets
- 3 or 4 tablespoons sesame seeds

Preheat oven to 350 degrees. Grease and flour a 13 × 9-inch pan.

Sift into a large bowl flour, baking powder, salt, and baking soda. Mix in the sugar, walnuts, sultanas, and orange peel.

In another bowl add the orange juice and water slowly to the tahini, blending thoroughly. (This may take patience. Some tahini is very thick and resistant to stirring.) Pour the tahini mixture into the flour mixture and stir well.

Spoon batter into the pan, spread it evenly, and sprinkle with sesame seeds. Bake for 45 to 50 minutes or until top of bread springs back. Cool in pan. If you like, you can dust the top with confectioner's sugar.

WALNUT BREAD

¶ *Walnuts are very popular but you may substitute other nuts such as almonds, pecans, filberts, or even pistachios in this recipe if you like. Try to imagine how the substitution will taste and alter the flavoring accordingly.*

1 LOAF

2½ cups unbleached flour, sifted
1 tablespoon baking powder
½ teaspoon salt
1 cup chopped walnuts
¼ cup (½ stick) unsalted butter, softened
¾ cup firmly packed dark brown sugar
1 egg
¾ cup plus 2 tablespoons milk
1 teaspoon vanilla

Preheat oven to 350 degrees. Grease an 8½ × 4½ × 2½-inch loaf pan.

Sift together into a bowl the flour, baking powder, and salt. Stir in the walnuts.

In a separate bowl cream the butter with the sugar until mixture is well blended. Beat in the egg and then the milk and vanilla. Beat in the flour mixture a little at a time until thoroughly mixed.

Spoon the batter into the pan.

Bake for 60 to 70 minutes or until a wooden pick inserted in center comes out clean. Allow bread to cool for 10 minutes on a wire rack. Remove from pan and allow to cool completely.

VEGETABLES

CARROT-PINEAPPLE-RAISIN BREAD

1 LOAF

1½ cups unbleached flour, sifted
  1 teaspoon baking powder
  ½ teaspoon baking soda
  ¼ teaspoon salt
  1 teaspoon cinnamon
  2 eggs
  ½ cup firmly packed light brown sugar
  ½ cup vegetable oil
  1 teaspoon vanilla
  ¾ cup chopped fresh or canned pineapple, well
     drained
  1 cup peeled and grated carrots
  ½ cup raisins

Preheat oven to 325 degrees. Grease and flour a 9 × 5 × 3-inch loaf pan.

Sift together the flour, baking powder, baking soda, salt, and cinnamon. Set aside.

In a large bowl beat the eggs. Add the sugar, oil, and vanilla, and mix well. Stir in the pineapple, carrots, and raisins.

Add the dry ingredients to the liquid mixture and stir just until well moistened.

Spoon batter into loaf pan and bake for 50 to 60 minutes or until a wooden pick inserted in center comes out clean. Cool on a rack for 10 minutes, remove from pan, and cool completely.

❧

PARSNIP BREAD

¶ *Don't dismiss this just because parsnips seem an un-usual ingredient in bread. The result is very tasty.*

2 Loaves

- 2 cups unbleached flour, sifted
- 1 teaspoon baking soda
- ½ teaspoon salt
- 1 cup whole wheat flour
- 2 cups cooked and mashed parsnips
- ½ cup grated carrots
- ½ cup yogurt
- ½ cup (1 stick) unsalted butter, softened
- 2 eggs, beaten
- 2 tablespoons chives
- 1 cup firmly packed brown sugar

Preheat oven to 350 degrees. Grease and flour two 9 × 5 × 3-inch loaf pans.

Sift together into a bowl the unbleached flour, baking soda, and salt. Then stir in the whole wheat flour.

In another bowl mix together the parsnips, carrots, yogurt, butter, and eggs and beat well to distribute the softened butter. To this mixture add the dry ingredients, chives, and brown sugar. Mix thoroughly.

Spoon into the loaf pans and bake for 1 hour. Cool on a rack for 10 minutes. Then remove from pans and cool thoroughly.

PUMPKIN NUT LOAF

¶ *Although we associate pumpkin primarily with the fall season and Thanksgiving, it is a delightful addition to a meal at any time of the year. The inclusion of cocoa makes this recipe unique.*

1 Loaf

- 2 cups unbleached flour, sifted
- 2 teaspoons baking powder
- 2 teaspoons cocoa
- 1 teaspoon cinnamon
- ½ teaspoon ginger
- ¼ teaspoon cloves
- ¼ teaspoon salt
- ¼ teaspoon baking soda
- 6 tablespoons (¾ stick) unsalted butter
- ⅔ cup light brown sugar
- 2 eggs
- 1 cup cooked and mashed pumpkin
- ¼ cup milk
- ¾ cup chopped filberts

Preheat oven to 350 degrees. Grease a 9 × 5 × 3-inch loaf pan.

Sift flour together with baking powder, cocoa, cinnamon, ginger, cloves, salt, and baking soda into a bowl.

In a large bowl cream the butter with the sugar until the mixture is light and fluffy. Beat in eggs, one at a time. Stir in the pumpkin.

Gradually stir the flour mixture into the pumpkin mixture alternately with the milk. Stir in the walnuts.

Pour the batter into the prepared pan and bake for 55 minutes or until a wooden pick inserted in the center comes out clean. Cool the bread in the pan for 10 minutes. Turn it out to cool completely on a wire rack.

SWEET POTATO BREAD

¶ *This Southern specialty has found a welcome home all over the United States. With the resurgence of enthusiasm for American regional cooking it is now appearing on restaurant menus as well.*

1 LOAF

2 cups unbleached flour, sifted
½ teaspoon salt
2 teaspoons baking powder
¼ teaspoon baking soda
1 teaspoon cinnamon
½ cup (1 stick) unsalted butter
⅔ cup granulated sugar
1 egg, beaten
1 cup cooked and mashed sweet potatoes
½ cup milk
½ cup chopped pecans

Preheat oven to 350 degrees. Grease a 9 × 5 × 3-inch loaf pan.

Sift together the flour, salt, baking powder, baking soda, and cinnamon. Set aside.

In a large bowl cream the butter until smooth. Add sugar gradually and beat until light and fluffy. Add the beaten egg and stir thoroughly. Then add sweet potatoes and mix well. Alternately add the dry ingredients and the milk, beating until everything is blended. Fold in pecans.

Pour into loaf pan and bake for 45 to 50 minutes. Cool for 10 minutes and remove from pan to cool thoroughly on a wire rack. This bread freezes well.

❧

ZUCCHINI BREAD

¶ *Every summer my father's garden is filled to the brim with vegetables. No matter how much he cuts back on his plantings, however, the overabundance is shared with neighbors and friends. My mother has invented dozens of uses for the multitude of zucchini that keep coming from that garden, and here is just one of her excellent zucchini breads.*

2 LOAVES

- 2 cups unpeeled grated zucchini (about 2 or 3 medium-sized)
- 1 cup raisins
- 3 cups unbleached flour
- 1 tablespoon cinnamon
- 1 teaspoon baking soda
- 1 teaspoon salt
- ¾ teaspoon baking powder
- 4 eggs
- 1 cup granulated sugar
- 1 cup vegetable oil
- 1 cup chopped walnuts
- 2 teaspoons grated lemon peel

Preheat oven to 350 degrees. Grease and flour two 9 × 5 × 3-inch loaf pans.

Grate zucchini, squeeze out as much liquid as possible, measure, and set aside.

Rinse raisins; drain. Mix with 2 tablespoons flour.

Sift flour. Resift with cinnamon, baking soda, salt, and baking powder.

In a large bowl beat eggs. Gradually beat in sugar, then oil. Add in dry ingredients alternately with zucchini and blend thoroughly. Stir in raisins, walnuts, and lemon peel.

Spoon into pans. Bake for 55 to 60 minutes or until top springs back when lightly touched. Cool in pans for 10 minutes. Turn out on wire racks to cool. This bread freezes well.

✿ ✿ ✿

A SAMPLING
OF OTHER
BAKED GOODS

CURRY CHEESE BISCUITS

¶ *Cheddar cheese is suggested for this recipe, but Colby or longhorn would make a milder and yet just as appealing biscuit.*

ABOUT 12 BISCUITS

¾ cup all-purpose flour, sifted
½ teaspoon baking powder
2 teaspoons curry powder
¼ cup (½ stick) unsalted butter
¼ cup grated sharp Cheddar cheese
1 egg yolk
2 tablespoons milk
¼ teaspoon salt
⅛ teaspoon dry mustard

Preheat oven to 400 degrees. Grease a baking sheet.

Sift together into a bowl the flour, baking powder, and curry powder. Cut in the butter with a pastry cutter or two knives until mixture resembles coarse corn meal. Add the grated cheese.

In another bowl mix together the egg yolk, milk, salt, and mustard. Pour into the flour mixture and blend thoroughly with a fork to make a soft dough. Turn out on a floured board and knead briefly. Roll out to ¼-inch thickness and cut into rounds with a biscuit cutter.

Arrange on a buttered baking sheet and bake at 400 degrees for 12 minutes.

HAM BISCUITS

¶ *These are a cross between a biscuit and a muffin, and they are fine partners for hot soup, especially lentil soup or black bean soup. Use any type of cooked ham that is available—boiled or baked.*

6 BISCUITS

¼ cup bread crumbs
3 tablespoons butter
4 eggs, separated
¾ cup sour cream
¼ cup grated mild Cheddar cheese
1 cup diced cooked ham

Preheat oven to 350 degrees. Grease a baking sheet.

Combine the bread crumbs, butter, egg yolks, sour cream, cheese, and ham in a large bowl.

In a clean bowl with clean beaters beat the egg whites until they are stiff. Gently fold the egg whites into the batter.

Drop by spoonfuls onto the baking sheet. Bake for 15 minutes or until lightly browned.

TEA BISCUITS

¶ *Tea biscuits are just what the name implies—biscuits to be served with afternoon tea. Serve them hot with jam, jelly, marmalade, or honey.*

14-16 2½-INCH BISCUITS

2 cups all-purpose flour
⅔ cup granulated sugar
1 teaspoon salt
4 teaspoons baking powder
1 cup whipping cream

Preheat oven to 450 degrees. Lightly grease a cookie sheet.

Sift flour. Resift into a bowl with sugar, salt, and baking powder.

Whip cream until thick. Blend cream with flour mixture.

Turn dough out on a lightly floured board and pat about ½-inch thick. Cut with a very small biscuit cutter and place on baking sheet. Bake for 10 to 12 minutes, until puffed and brown.

GINGERBREAD

1½ cups unbleached flour, sifted
½   teaspoon baking soda
½   teaspoon baking powder
½   teaspoon salt
½   cup packed light brown sugar
1   teaspoon ground ginger
1   teaspoon cinnamon
¼   teaspoon allspice
¼   teaspoon nutmeg
¼   cup (½ stick) unsalted butter, melted
¼   cup maple syrup
½   cup sour milk (see note)
1   egg, beaten

Preheat oven to 350 degrees. Grease an 8-inch square cake pan.

Sift together into a large bowl the flour, baking soda, baking powder, and salt. Add the sugar and spices and blend thoroughly.

In a small bowl, stir the melted butter with the maple syrup, sour milk, and egg until thoroughly mixed.

Add the liquid ingredients to the dry ingredients and beat until the batter is smooth, approximately 2 to 3 minutes.

Spoon batter into pan and bake for 30 to 35 minutes or until gingerbread springs back when lightly touched. Serve warm with a sauce or vanilla bean ice cream.

NOTE: If you have no sour milk on hand, simply stir 1 tablespoon vinegar or lemon juice into a scant ½ cup sweet milk, let stand a few minutes until the surface ruffles, and stir.

PECAN SHORTBREAD

ABOUT 16 WEDGES

1 cup (2 sticks) unsalted butter, softened
½ cup granulated sugar
½ cup finely chopped pecans (preferably done in a
   blender or food processor)
1 teaspoon vanilla
¼ teaspoon salt
2 cups unbleached flour, sifted

Preheat oven to 325 degrees. Grease a 9-inch round cake pan.

Cream the butter and sugar together until light and fluffy. Add the nuts, vanilla, and salt and blend well. Add the flour and beat thoroughly. The dough will be heavy.

Spoon the dough into the cake pan. Smooth the top out level as the dough won't change shape while baking. Bake for 40 to 45 minutes or until lightly browned. Cool in pan. Then cut into wedges.

POPOVERS 1

¶ *There are a few simple suggestions to keep in mind when baking popovers. First, all ingredients should be at room temperature before you start to assemble the batter. Next, beat or mix only until the ingredients have been thoroughly blended. Don't overdo it. And finally, once the popovers are in the oven don't be tempted to open the door. Let them bake the allotted time.*

12 POPOVERS

¾ cup (12 tablespoons) grated Parmesan cheese
3 eggs
1 cup milk
1 cup sifted all-purpose flour
½ teaspoon salt

Preheat oven to 425 degrees. Generously grease the bottoms and sides of popover or muffin pans.

Put one tablespoon of cheese into the bottom of each pan.

Beat eggs until light and fluffy. Add the milk, flour, and salt and mix just until smooth.

Fill cups and bake for 40 minutes. The popovers should be crisp and brown. If they are not, bake another 5 minutes. Serve immediately.

POPOVERS 2 AND VARIATIONS

¶ *Many experts suggest preheating the greased popover pans for extra height and crispness.*

12 POPOVERS

2 eggs
1 cup milk
1 tablespoon unsalted butter, melted
½ teaspoon salt
1 cup unbleached flour, sifted

Preheat oven to 425 degrees. Grease popover pans thoroughly.

Beat eggs. Add milk, butter, and salt. Mix in flour until batter is smooth. Then beat 3 minutes by hand or 1 minute by electric hand mixer.

Pour batter into popover pans. Bake 40 to 45 minutes or until well puffed and brown. For a crisper popover, prick the side of each popover with a fork, lower the oven temperature to 350 degrees and bake for an additional 20 minutes. Serve hot.

POPOVER VARIATIONS

Bacon Popovers: Fry or broil 3 strips of bacon until crisp. Drain thoroughly on paper towels. Substitute 1 tablespoon bacon drippings for butter in basic recipe. Crumble bacon over batter in popover pan.

Almond Popover: Pulverize 1½ tablespoons almonds in a blender. Crumble them on top of popover batter and bake as in basic recipe.

Cheese Popovers: Blend ⅓ cup grated or shredded sharp Cheddar cheese or Parmesan cheese into the egg mixture.

SOUR CREAM COFFEE CAKE

ONE 9-INCH CAKE

2 cups minus two tablespoons unbleached flour, sifted
1 teaspoon baking powder
1 teaspoon baking soda
¼ teaspoon salt
2 eggs
½ cup (1 stick) unsalted butter, softened
½ cup brown sugar
1 teaspoon vanilla extract
1 cup sour cream

TOPPING:
1 cup chopped pecans
¼ cup (½ stick) unsalted butter, melted
⅓ cup brown sugar
1 teaspoon cinnamon

Preheat oven to 350 degrees. Grease a 9-inch spring form pan or a 9-inch square pan.

Sift flour, baking powder, baking soda, and salt. Sift again.

Beat eggs in a large bowl. Add the butter, sugar, and vanilla and beat well, until softened butter is completely incorporated. Add half the sour cream and half the flour mixture and mix thoroughly. Add the remaining sour cream and flour and again mix thoroughly.

Pour half the batter into the pan.

Mix together the topping ingredients and sprinkle half the topping on the batter. Pour on the remaining batter. Sprinkle the remaining topping mixture over the batter as evenly as possible.

Bake 45 to 55 minutes or until a wooden pick comes out clean. Cool in the pan for 10 minutes before cutting or removing from pan.

❦   ❦   ❦

SAUCES
AND
SPREADS

HOMEMADE YOGURT

¶ As long as I can remember my parents have made yogurt in our home. It is made the way it was in Levidi, my father's town in Greece, and probably it was made this way in my maternal grandparents' villages.

Although yogurt in all forms is readily available in retail outlets, it is worth learning how to make if you use it frequently. There are expensive commercial yogurt makers on the market but this simple method needs no special equipment.

My brother and I had an aversion to standing patiently and stirring the milk over a flame in the kitchen (particularly if the weather beckoned us outside) so we became adept at fleeing if we saw my father arriving with a full gallon of milk.

For many years we were able to get raw milk from a local farmer but as commercialization of the area grew this became impossible. Pasteurized milk will work just fine.

Here is my father's recipe for yogurt.

1 gallon milk
2 to 3 tablespoons starter (leftover plain yogurt from the previous batch or *plain* commercial yogurt)
½ cup milk

EQUIPMENT NEEDED:
Large kettle with a lid
Several wool blankets
A muslin or 100 percent cotton bag or pillowcase
String

Bring the gallon of milk to the boiling point, stirring constantly, preferably with a wooden spoon.

Allow milk to cool to the point where you can dip your finger in and leave it there while you count to twelve (about 106° to 109° F.). If the milk is much cooler or hotter than this, the yogurt is likely to fail.

In a separate bowl or glass measuring cup stir two tablespoons of starter into the ½ cup of plain milk. Make sure that the mixture is blended well. Add to the boiled milk and stir in thoroughly.

Cover the kettle and place in a warm area with no drafts. Place one blanket under the kettle and bring the blanket up around it. Place a second blanket on top of this. All of the kettle should be completely covered. Allow the yogurt to sit undisturbed in a draft-free place overnight or for at least 8 to 10 hours.

As soon as the yogurt is ready, pour the contents of the kettle into the muslin bag. (Do this over the sink to catch any spills.) Tie bag securely and hang for 1 hour or more over a sink or container that the yogurt can drain into. The length of time that the yogurt drains will determine how thick the mixture becomes—if a thinner yogurt is desired, do not allow to drain longer than 45 minutes to an hour. If you want a thicker product allow it to drain several hours.

After yogurt has drained to desired consistency, empty contents of muslin bag into a glass or earthenware bowl. Cover and store in refrigerator. This yogurt will keep well at least a week to 10 days. It can be eaten plain or with fruit and/or nuts, or used in cooking.

APPLESAUCE-YOGURT SAUCE

¶ *This is a rich sauce, but not nearly as caloric as other toppings. Serve it chilled.*

2½ CUPS

1 cup fresh applesauce
1 cup yogurt
¼ cup mild honey, such as clover
⅓ cup finely ground walnuts

Mix with a beater the applesauce, yogurt, and honey until mixture is smooth. Then mix in the finely ground walnuts.

ALMOND BUTTER

1 CUP

2½ ounces blanched almonds (see note on blanching nuts)
    A few drops cold water
10 tablespoons (one stick plus 2 tablespoons) unsalted butter, softened

Place almonds in blender and process at high speed, adding a few drops of cold water as necessary to keep nuts from becoming too oily. When mixture is smooth, add the softened butter and mix thoroughly.
    Chill until ready to use.

NOTE: To blanch almonds, plunge shelled almonds into boiling water for a few seconds until the skins expand and loosen. Drain and then pinch the kernels free.

BASIL BUTTER

¶ *This basil butter goes well with the chickpea muffins on page 19 or the rice muffins on page 28.*

5 TABLESPOONS

¼ cup (½ stick) unsalted butter, softened
2 teaspoons finely chopped shallots
1 tablespoon lemon juice
¼ cup chopped fresh basil leaves

Cream all ingredients together until well blended.

HONEY BUTTERS

¶ *The following recipes are excellent to serve with muffin and bread recipes as well as waffles, pancakes, and French toast. Using these proportions as a basis, try whatever fruit substitutes appeal to you.*

GOLDEN HONEY BUTTER

1 CUP

½ cup (1 stick) unsalted butter, softened
¾ cup honey

Whip the butter in an electric mixer on a low speed until it is light and fluffy. Add the honey slowly, beating all the time, until the two ingredients are well blended.

This should be used at room temperature, but refrigerate any leftovers.

CHERRY HONEY

1 Cup

1 cup large sour cherries, pitted carefully to preserve
   the shape of the cherry
¾ cup honey

Heat the honey over a low flame. Add the cherries and
simmer for 3 to 5 minutes, stirring gently from time to
time.

Cool and store in refrigerator if not used immediately.
This mixture cannot be kept for long periods. It should be
used within a week or two of preparation.

ORANGE HONEY

1½ Cups

1 cup honey
⅓ cup unsalted butter, softened
   Juice of 1 orange (about ⅓ cup)
   Grated rind of 1 orange (1½ tablespoons)

Blend all the ingredients together. Keep unused portion
in refrigerator.

LIME BUTTER

¼ Cup

¼ cup (½ stick) unsalted butter
   Grated rind of 1 lime
1 tablespoon lime juice

Cream the butter. Add the grated rind and lime juice and
blend until smooth.

This is very good spread on thin slice of any type of nut
bread.

HONEY-NUT SPREAD

1½ Cups

¾ cup whipped butter
½ cup crunchy peanut butter
⅓ cup honey

Stir all ingredients until well blended.

VANILLA SAUCE

2 Cups

½ cup granulated sugar
 2 tablespoons cornstarch
¼ teaspoon salt
 2 cups boiling water
¼ cup (½ stick) unsalted butter
 2 tablespoons vanilla

Combine sugar, cornstarch, and salt in a saucepan. Slowly add boiling water, stirring constantly until smooth. Simmer for 5 to 7 minutes. Remove from heat. Add butter. Cool for 5 minutes and add vanilla.

Serve warm over apple bread or chocolate bread.

APPENDIX

EQUIVALENT WEIGHTS AND MEASURES

Almonds	6 oz.	equals	1 cup
Apples	1 medium	"	1 cup sliced
	1 lb.	"	3 medium apples
Apricots, fresh	1 lb.	"	3 cups, pitted
dried	1 lb.	"	3 cups
Baking powder	1 oz.	"	3 tablespoons
Bananas, mashed	1 lb.	"	2 cups
Berries	1 quart	"	3½ cups
Butter	1 oz.	"	2 tablespoons
	½ cup	"	8 tablespoons or 1 stick
	1 lb.	"	2 cups
Cashews, shelled	1 lb.	"	4 cups
Cheese, cottage	8 oz.	"	1 cup
cream	3 oz.	"	6 tablespoons
cream	1 lb.	"	2 cups
Chocolate, grated	1 oz.	"	4 tablespoons
melted	8 oz.	"	1 cup
Cocoa	1 oz.	"	4 tablespoons

EQUIVALENT WEIGHTS AND MEASURES

Coconut, flaked	3½ oz.	"	1⅓ cups
Corn meal, uncooked	1 cup	"	4 cups cooked
Cornstarch	1 oz.	"	3 tablespoons
Cranberries	1 lb.	"	4 cups
Cream, heavy	1 cup	"	2 cups, whipped
Cream of tartar	1 oz.	"	3 tablespoons
Currants, dried	1 lb.	"	3 cups
Dates, pitted	1 lb.	"	2½ cups
Egg, whole	1	"	3 tablespoons, approx.
	5 medium	"	1 cup
Egg whites	8 to 10	"	1 cup
Egg yolks	12 to 16	"	1 cup
Figs, dried & chopped	1 lb.	"	2¾ cups
Filberts or hazelnuts	1 lb.	"	3½ cups
Flour, all-purpose or unbleached	1 lb.	"	4 cups
Flour, cake	1 lb.	"	4 cups
Honey	11 oz.	"	1 cup
Lemon, whole	4 medium	"	1 lb.
	1 medium	"	2 to 3 table-spoons juice
grated	1 medium	"	1 to 2 table-spoons
rind	1 medium	"	2 tablespoons, approx.
Lime	1 medium	"	1½ to 2 table-spoons juice
Milk, whole	8 oz.	"	1 cup
Molasses	12 oz.	"	1 cup
Oatmeal	1 lb.	"	2⅔ cups
Oats, rolled	1 lb.	"	4¾ cups

EQUIVALENT WEIGHTS AND MEASURES

Orange	1 medium	"	½ cup chopped
	1 medium	"	⅓ to ½ cup juice
grated	1 medium	"	3 tablespoons
peel	1 medium	"	2 to 3 table-spoons
Peaches, dried	1 lb.	"	3 cups
fresh & sliced	1 lb.	"	2 cups
Peanuts	5 ozs.	"	1 cup
Pecans, shelled	1 lb.	"	4 cups
Pineapple, diced	1 lb.	"	2 cups
Prunes	1 lb.	"	3 cups
Raisins, seedless	1 lb.	"	3 cups
Rhubarb, sliced	1 lb.	"	2¼ cups
Salt	1 oz.	"	1¾ tablespoons
Soda, baking	1 oz.	"	2½ tablespoons
Strawberries, whole	1 quart	"	3½ cups
Sugar, brown	1 lb.	"	3 cups
confectioner's	1 lb.	"	3½ cups
granulated	1 lb.	"	2 cups
Vanilla extract	1 oz.	"	2 tablespoons
Walnuts, shelled	1 lb.	"	4 cups

INDEX

A

Almond butter, 127
Almond-lime loaf, 82–83
Apple bread, fresh, 84
Apple-date loaf, 85
Apple muffins, 29
Apple cheese muffins, 30
Applesauce bread, 73–74
Applesauce-yogurt sauce,
     127
Apricot bran bread, 74–75
Apricot-nut muffins, 42–
     43

B

Baking
   equipment for, 4–5
   guidelines for success,
     6–9
   ingredients, 10–12

Banana-date bread, 86
Banana-date muffins, 31
Banana-pistachio bread,
     87
Biscuits
   curry cheese biscuits,
     115
   ham biscuits, 116
   tea biscuits, 117
Blueberry muffins, 32–33
Blueberry-orange bread,
     76–77
Bran muffins, 16–17
   with cream cheese and
     orange marmalade, 18
Breads
   brown bread, 65–66
   chocolate bread, 66–67
   cinnamon bread, 68
   corn bread, 68–69
   graham bread, 69–70
   oatmeal-raisin bread,
     70–71

spoon bread, 71
swoop bread, 72
See also Fruit breads;
    Fruit/nut breads; Nut/
    seed breads; Vegetable
    breads.
Butters
    almond butter, 127
    basic butter, 128
    basil butter, 128
    cherry honey butter, 129
    golden honey butter,
        128–29
    lime butter, 129
    orange honey butter, 129

C

Carrot-pineapple-raisin
    bread, 106–7
Carrot-zucchini muffins,
    46–47
Cherry bread, 88–89
Cherry honey, 129
Cherry muffins, 34
Chickpea muffins, 19–20
Chocolate bread, 66–67
Cinnamon bread, 68
Coconut muffins, 59–60
Coffee cake, sour cream,
    122
Coffee muffins, 60
Corn bread, 68–69
Corn muffins
    basic, 20
    blue corn meal, 22
    cheesy, 21
    jalapeño, 23

raspberry, 24
Cranberry muffins, 35
Cranberry nut bread, 91
Cranberry-orange pecan
    bread, 90
Curry cheese biscuits, 115

D

Date muffins, 43
Date nut bread, 92
Dried fruit muffins
    apricot-nut muffins, 42–
        43
    date muffins, 43
    fig muffins, 44
    prune muffins, 45

F

Fig muffins, 44
Flours, types of, 10–11
Fruit breads
    applesauce bread, 73–74
    apricot bran bread, 74–
        75
    blueberry-orange bread,
        76–77
    kiwi bread, 77–78
    lemon bread, 78–79
    plum bread, 79–80
    spirited, 99
    strawberry bread, 80–81
Fruit muffins
    apple cheese muffins, 30
    apple muffins, 29
    banana-date muffins, 31

blueberry muffins, 32–33

cherry muffins, 34

cranberry muffins, 35

grapefruit muffins, 36

lemon muffins, 37

peach muffins, 38

pear muffins, 39

pineapple-bacon muffins, 40

strawberry yogurt muffins, 41

Fruit/nut breads

almond-lime loaf, 82–83

apple bread, 84

apple-date loaf, 85

banana-date bread, 86

banana-pistachio bread, 87

cherry bread, 88–89

cranberry-orange pecan bread, 90

cranberry nut bread, 91

date nut bread, 92

fruit bread, spirited, 99

honey-prune bread, 93

orange-date bread, 95

orange-oatmeal bread, 94

pecan-raisin bread, 96

pineapple-coconut bread, 97

rhubarb bread, 98

G

Ginger muffins, 56–57

Gingerbread, 118

Golden honey butter, 128–29

Graham bread, 69–70

Graham muffins, 25

Grapefruit muffins, 36

H

Ham biscuits, 116

Health nut muffins, 50–51

Honey butters, 128–29

Honey-nut spread, 130

Honey-prune bread, 93

J

Jelly muffins (muffins with a surprise), 61–62

K

Kiwi bread, 77–78

L

Lemon bread, 78–79

Lemon muffins, 37

Lime butter, 129

M

Maple filbert muffins, 51–52

Maple walnut bread, 100–101

Muffins
  basic, 15–16
  bran muffins, 16–17
  bran muffins with cream
    cheese and orange
    marmalade, 18
  chickpea muffins, 19–20
  coconut muffins, 59–60
  coffee muffins, 60
  corn muffins
    basic, 20
    blue corn meal, 22
    cheesy, 21
    jalapeño, 23
    raspberry, 24
  graham muffins, 25
  jelly muffins (muffins
    with a surprise), 61–
    62
  oatmeal muffins, 26
  rice muffins, 28
  Sally Lunn, 62
  wheat muffins, orange,
    27
  See also Dried fruit
    muffins; Fruit muffins;
    Nut/seed muffins;
    Spice muffins;
    Vegetable muffins.

N

Nut loaf, 101–2
Nutmeg muffins, 57–58
Nut/seed breads
  maple walnut bread,
    100–101
  nut loaf, 101–2

peanut butter bread,
    102–3
  tahini (sesame) bread,
    104
  walnut bread, 105
Nut/seed muffins
  health nut muffins, 50–
    51
  maple filbert muffins,
    51–52
  pecan spice muffins, 52
  pine nut-raisin muffins,
    53
  poppy seed muffins, 54
  sunny seeded muffins,
    55

O

Oatmeal muffins, 26
Oatmeal-raisin bread, 70–
    71
Orange honey, 129
Orange-date bread, 95
Orange-oatmeal bread, 94

P

Parsnip bread, 107–8
Peach muffins, 38
Peanut butter bread, 102–
    3
Pear muffins, 39
Pecan shortbread, 119
Pecan spice muffins, 52
Pecan-raisin bread, 96
Pine nut-raisin muffins, 53

Pineapple-bacon muffins, 40
Pineapple-coconut bread, 97
Plum bread, 79–80
Popovers, 120–21
Poppy seed muffins, 54
Prune muffins, 45
Pumpkin muffins, 47–48
Pumpkin nut loaf, 108–9

R

Rhubarb bread, 98
Rice muffins, 28

S

Sally Lunn, 62
Sauces/spreads
    almond butter, 127
    applesauce-yogurt sauce, 127
    basil butter, 128
    cherry honey, 129
    golden honey butter, 128–29
    honey-nut spread, 130
    lime butter, 129
    orange honey, 129
    vanilla sauce, 130
    yogurt homemade, 125–26
Sesame (tahini) bread, 104
Shortbread, pecan, 119
Sour cream coffee cake, 122

Spice muffins
    ginger muffins, 56–57
    nutmeg muffins, 57–58
Spoon bread, 71
Spreads, *See* Sauces/spreads.
Squash muffins, 48–49
Strawberry bread, 80–81
Strawberry yogurt muffins, 41
Sunny seeded muffins, 55
Sweet potato bread, 109–10
Swoop bread, 72

T

Tahini (sesame) bread, 104
Tea biscuits, 117

V

Vanilla sauce, 130
Vegetable breads
    carrot-pineapple-raisin bread, 106–7
    parsnip bread, 107–8
    pumpkin nut loaf, 108–9
    sweet potato bread, 109–10
    zucchini bread, 110–11
Vegetable muffins
    carrot-zucchini muffins, 46–47
    pumpkin muffins, 47–48
    squash muffins, 48–49

zucchini muffins with
    wheat germ, 49

W

Walnut bread, 105
Wheat muffins, orange, 27

Y

Yogurt
  applesauce-yogurt sauce,
    127
homemade, 125–26

Z

Zucchini bread, 110–11
Zucchini muffins with
    wheat germ, 49

❦   ❦   ❦

ABOUT THE AUTHOR

DIMETRA MAKRIS *is the author of* First Prize Quilts, *and co-author (with Diane Powell and David Dax) of* First Prize Cookbook. *A first generation Greek-American, Dimetra learned to cook at a young age from her mother, a Greek cooking instructor. She makes her home in New York City.*